F1 93

F. 1 '93

Testi/Text
Tom Roberts

Fotografie/Photographs
Bryn Williams

Grafica/Graphics
Maurizio Belardinelli - Graziano Pedrocchi

Coordinamento Tecnico/Technical Coordinator
Giuseppe Malorni

Fotolito/Photolithography
Fratelli Colombo fotolito - Milano

Stampa/Printer
Tiber - Brescia

Realizzazione
Vallardi & Associati - Milano

© Vallardi & Associati - Milano

Finito di stampare nel Novembre 1993
in Italia

Produced by Vallardi & Associati - Milano

Printed in Italy

Printing completed: November 1993, Milano

© Vallardi & Associati (Milano) 1993

ISBN 88-85202-27-6

Bryn Williams
ha maturato la sua
considerevole esperienza
di fotografo nel settore
dell'automobilismo
lavorando per la B.B.C.
in Inghilterra e per molte
agenzie e riviste
di tutto il mondo
fin dal 1983.
E' direttore
dell'agenzia stampa
Words & Pictures, che ha
costituito nel 1990
con altri giornalisti
e fotografi professionisti
allo scopo di elaborare
materiale adatto
alla pubblicazione
in tutto il mondo.
L'agenzia ha sede
a Oxford proprio
nei pressi delle squadre
inglesi di F.1:
la Williams, la Benetton
e la Jordan.
Bryn utilizza
apparecchiature Canon
da 35mm e ha seguito
l'intero campionato
mondiale del 1993
per la Vallardi & Associati.
Le sue stupende immagini
illustrano
il nostro libro sulla
Formula Uno del 1993.

All photographs in this book
have been taken
with camera equipment of

Canon

*Bryn Williams has gained
considerable experience
as a photographer
in the world
of Grand Prix racing,
having worked
for the BBC in England
and many agencies
and magazines
worldwide since 1983.
He is Managing Director
of the Media agency
Words & Pictures,
which he formed in
1990, consisting of
professional journalists
and photographers
all dedicated to providing
written and photographic
material to publications
throughout the world.
The agency is based
near Oxford, England
and located close
to the Williams,
Benetton and Jordan
Grand Prix teams.
Bryn uses Canon
35mm equipment
and has attended
the entire 1992 F1
World Championship
for Vallardi & Associati.
His superb photography
illustrates
our 1993 F1 Annual.*

Tom Roberts
vive tra Londra
ed il Galles del Nord.
Giornalista indipendente,
ha collaborato
con l'agenzia stampa
Words & Pictures,
si è occupato
di automobilismo
(Formula Uno,
Formula 3000
e automobili da turismo),
ha infine redatto
numerosi articoli per
la stampa internazionale.
Tom Roberts
è anche socio
in una società di ricerca.

*Tom Roberts
lives in London
and North Wales.
He is a freelance
journalist who has
written for the media
agency Words & Pictures.
He has covered F1,
F3000 and Touring Cars,
as well as contributing
feature articles to many
foreign publications.
He is also a partner
in a leading London
based transportation
research company.*

Il 1993 ha visto il rientro di Alain Prost in Formula Uno e la profezia che il pilota francese e la Williams-Renault avrebbero dominato la stagione si è ampiamente avverata. Se non fosse stato per le superbe prestazioni di Ayrton Senna, che ha conquistato ben cinque vittorie in Gran Premio, si sarebbe creata una situazione analoga a quella del 1992, quando Mansell aveva stravinto. Il timore che la recessione economica mondiale avrebbe tagliato le gambe anche alla Formula Uno si è rivelato fortunatamente esagerato. Tutte le squadre, fatta eccezione per la Scuderia Italia, sono arrivate fino in fondo e la fine del Campionato del mondo delle Sports Car ha portato in Gran Premio una nuova squadra, quella della Sauber, con cui la Mercedes ha sondato il terreno della Formula Uno.

Quando Prost è ritornato alla Formula Uno, era opinione diffusa che non sarebbe riuscito a vincere il Campionato del Mondo. Si trattava di Prost, guidava una Williams-Renault, il campione in carica aveva abbandonato la Formula Uno e il suo compagno di squadra non aveva esperienza in queste gare. Ma fin dall'inizio per Prost vincere il suo quarto titolo non è stato semplice. Prima che le luci divenissero verdi a Kyalami, si era trovato coinvolto in una disputa con la FISA. Le considerazioni che Prost aveva fatto a proposito della FISA su una rivista lo avevano trascinato davanti al tribunale. In seguito la faccenda è sfumata, ma tra i due contendenti è rimasta una tensione costante. Prost si è sentito perseguitato in più di una occasione: a Monaco e in Germania per le penalità inflittegli e, più tardi, anche a Estoril dove l'annuncio del suo ritiro ha scatenato l'esplosione di Bernie Ecclestone della Foca , manifestazione sotto cui il pilota ha visto l'ostilità dell'intero gruppo dirigente. Durante tutta la stagione Prost ha mantenuto l'intima convinzione che le regole non venissero applicate equamente e che egli fosse stato designato vittima principale. Osservando i fatti non si può dargli torto.

Il rifugio di Prost è stata la sua squadra, la Williams, con cui ha celebrato una delle sue stagioni più felici, mentre i ricordi dei turbolenti anni alla Ferrari e alla McLaren sono pian piano sbiaditi. La convivenza con il suo compagno di squadra Damon Hill è stata all'insegna del reciproco rispetto. La sfilza di pole position che Prost si è accaparrato e il suo modo di guidare pulito e controllato, rilevabile soprattutto nel Gran Premio del Canada, spiegano quale sia la sua tecnica per affrontare le gare.e i rivali. Questi non gli sono certo mancati: i più temibili sono stati senz'altro Senna, Schumacher e l'ambizioso Hill, "sbocciato" e rafforzatosi proprio sotto la tutela di Prost.

La decisione di Prost di ritirarsi come campione in carica è stata accolta con sorpresa, anche se il pilota è apparso stanco. Detiene un record quasi senza precedenti, con 51 vittorie in Gran Premio e più punti di qualsiasi altro pilota nella storia di questo sport. Solo il leggendario Fangio ha più titoli mondiali di Prost, essendo diventato Campione del Mondo ben cinque volte. I suoi progetti futuri rimangono ancora un mistero; gira la voce che avrà incarichi manageriali. Dopo il contrasto Irvine-Senna verificatosi in Giappone, la richiesta di un giudice-pilota per la Formula Uno si è fatta più insistente. Date la sua esperienza e la sua intelligenza, sarebbe quantomeno interessante se fosse Prost a ricoprire questo ruolo.

Il 1993 avrebbe potuto essere l'ultima stagione di gloria per i piloti della vecchia guardia, ma la generazione più giovane ha dimostrato di averli rapidamente raggiunti. I piloti destinati a essere i migliori in questa nuova era sembrano Schumacher, Hill e Hakkinen, ma in questa stagione si sono messi in luce con sorprendenti prestazioni anche due debuttanti, Rubens Barricchello e Eddie Irvine.

Molti hanno lamentato che il 1992 era stata una stagione monotona. La FISA ha cambiato le regole per il 1993 per contenere la velocità, ma i cambiamenti non hanno impedito a Prost e a Hill di surclassare molti risultati ottenuti da Mansell nella stagione precedente. In Canada si è avuta un'anticipazione delle intenzioni della FISA. Il corpo dirigente del Gran Premio, forse spronato dalle crescenti rivelazioni della Formula Indy, ha stabilito nuove regole per il 1994 per ribadire l'importanza predominante del pilota sull'auto. Il pubblico può solo accettare le intenzioni della FISA. Poiché la ricerca si dirige verso innovazioni tecnologiche sempre più sofisticate, non è un male che il pilota diventi un vero e proprio "tecnico". La Formula Uno è tradizionalmente un settore in cui viene impiegata tecnologia ad alti livelli. Bandire molti dei sistemi impiegati non renderà le gare automaticamente più eccitanti, ma se i costi proibitivi dello sviluppo tecnologico venissero tagliati, il divario tra chi si può permettere di sostenere grosse spese e chi non può farlo si assottiglierebbe. C'è chi teme che l'interesse dei costruttori per le innovazioni diventi più debole a causa delle restrizioni. In realtà sembra che gli acquirenti per il 1994 non manchino. La Peugeot debutterà in Formula Uno e la Honda, dopo il suo ritiro nel 1992, sta pianificando un rientro con Mugen nella squadra della Lotus. É un peccato che la politica della Formula Uno abbia fatto fuggire la Chrysler.

Nel preparare questo testo, ho cercato di adottare uno schema particolare, adatto a riflettere sulle gare dell'anno. Per ogni Gran Premio è stato prescelto un pilota che illustra la sua immagine della gara. Le opinioni di ogni protagonista sono accompagnate dalle superbe fotografie di Bryn Williams. Una parte tecnica, infine, si occupa dei principali traguardi tecnologici raggiunti nella Formula Uno.

Tom Roberts

Novembre 1993

1993 heralded the return of Alain Prost to F1 and the prophesy that he and Williams-Renault would dominate the season proved largely true. Were it not for the superlative driving skills of Ayrton Senna, who in gaining five GP victories hardly put a wheel wrong, the season could have been the whitewash that was 1992 when Mansell dominated. Fears that the world wide recession would cut the legs from under the sport fortunately proved exaggerated. All the teams, bar Scuderia Italia, completed the season and the demise of the World Sports Car Championship brought a new team in the form of Sauber, a vehicle for Mercedes to test the F1 waters.

When Prost returned to F1 following his years sabbatical the prevailing view was that he could not win the World Championship, only lose it. He was Prost, he had a Williams-Renault, the reigning World Champion had left F1 and his teammate was inexperienced. The reality was very different and from the beginning winning his fourth title was never going to be easy. Before the lights turned green at Kyalami, Prost found himself embroiled in a battle with FISA. Comments he made about FISA in a magazine saw him hauled up in front of a tribunal, charged with bringing the sport into disrepute and facing a possible ban. Things blew over, but there remained a perceptible undercurrent of tension between the two parties. Prost felt cheated after the stop-go penalties imposed at Monaco and Germany and further evidence of the feud with the governers of the sport came in the form of a remarkable outburst from FOCA boss Bernie Eccclestone following Prost's announcement at Estoril of his retirement. Throughout the season Prost maintained the view that the rules were applied unevenly and that he had been selected as prime victim. Looking at the plain facts one can sympathise with that view.

Prost's sanctuary was the Williams team, with whom he enjoyed one of his happiest seasons, as memories of turbulent years with Ferrari and McLaren faded. His relationship with his teammate Damon Hill was mutually respectful. His string of pole positions show how he made the most of his car's advantage and his trademark smooth and seemingly effortless driving was evident in his performances, especially at Canada. But he was not without challengers in the form of Senna, Schumacher and the ambitious Hill, who blossomed under the tutelage of Prost and gained confidence as the season progressed.

Prost's decision to retire as reigning World Champion was greeted with some surprise, but he appeared weary. He has an almost unparalleled record, with a remarkable 51 wins and more points than any other driver in the history of the sport. Only the legendary Fangio has more World Championship titles with five. His future plans remain unclear, with rumours flying about a future management role. Following the Senna-Irvine controversy at Japan, the call for a F1 driver-judge has grown louder. Given his wealth of experience and intelligent approach to the sport, it would be interesting, to say the least, if Prost were to take on that role.

1993 may have been the last season for the old guard, but a younger generation is coming swiftly up behind them. The obvious candidates to lead the new driver era are Schumacher, Hill and Hakkinen, but this season also saw impressive debut performances by Rubens Barrichello and Eddie Irvine.

Many complained that 1992 saw processional driving and that the season as a whole was dull. FISA changed the rules for 1993 in an attempt to slow the cars down, but wing size and tyre width were reduced to little effect. The changes did not prevent Prost and Hill eclipsing many of Mansell's best times from the previous season. More drastic steps were required and Canada saw an early indication of FISA's intentions. GP's governing body, perhaps spurred by the increasing exposure of the Indycar series, following Mansell's move, with its emphasis on wheel to wheel racing, has made further rule changes for 1994 in an attempt to reassert the importance of the driver over the car and make for closer racing. Spectators of the sport can only support FISA's aims. As more sophisticated levels of technology are within reach, there is a real danger of the driver becoming a mere technician in this "Brave New World". F1 has traditionally been a high technology training ground and banning many of the systems developed will not automatically bring more exciting racing, but if the prohibitive costs of development can be cut back, the performance gulf between the "haves" and the "have nots" may be narrowed. There are those who fear wavering interest on the part of manufacturers as a result of the restrictions placed on development, but there would appear to be no shortage of takers for 1994. Peugeot will make a welcome debut in F1 and Honda, after its withdrawal in 1992, are set to make a return through the backdoor with Mugen at Team Lotus. It is regretable that F1 politics would appear to have frightened off a Chrysler, crucial link with the U.S. in the form of Chrysler.

In putting together F1 '93, I have attempted to choose a different format with which to reflect on the year's racing. A driver has been selected to give his perspective of a particular race and his views are accompanied by Bryn Williams' superb photography. In addition there a features covering the main technological developments in F1.

Tom Roberts

November 1993

SOUTH AFRICA

The race of:

Christian Fittipaldi

14 March 1993 ● Circuit: Kyalami ● Length: 306,792 km ● Organiser: Kyalami Grand Prix Circuit ● Race Director: Roland Bruynseraede ● Spectators: 70.000 ● Weather: Friday and Saturday clear, Sunday clear and storm

🏁🏁🏁🏁🏁🏁🏁🏁🏁🏁🏁🏁🏁

A. Prost Williams 1'15"696 (202,647)	**A. Senna** McLaren 1'15"784 (202,412)
M. Schumacher Benetton 1'17"261 (198,543)	**D. Hill** Williams 1'17"592 (197,696)
J. Alesi Ferrari 1'18"234 (196,073)	**J.J. Lehto** Sauber 1'18"664 (195,002)
R. Patrese Benetton 1'18"676 (194,972)	**M. Blundell** Ligier 1'18"687 (194,945)
M. Andretti McLaren 1'18"786 (194,700)	**K. Wendlinger** Sauber 1'18"950 (194,295)
P. Alliot Larrousse 1'19"034 (194,089)	**M. Brundle** Ligier 1'19"138 (193,834)
C. Fittipaldi Minardi 1'19"285 (193,474)	**R. Barrichello** Jordan 1'19"305 (193,425)
G. Berger Ferrari 1'19"386 (193,228)	**A. Zanardi** Lotus 1'19"396 (193,204)
J. Herbert Lotus 1'19"498 (192,956)	**I. Capelli** Jordan 1'19"759 (192,324)
E. Comas Larrousse 1'20"081 (191,551)	**A. Suzuki** Footwork 1'20"237 (191,179)
U. Katayama Tyrrell 1'20"401 (190,789)	**D. Warwick** Footwork 1'20"402 (190,786)
A. De Cesaris Tyrrell 1'20"660 (190,176)	**F. Barbazza** Minardi 1'20"994 (189,392)
M. Alboreto Lola Bms 1'21"893 (187,313)	**L. Badoer** Lola Bms 1'24"737 (181,026)

After months of speculation and expectation many questions were answered at Kyalami. Two and a half years after his last GP victory Alain Prost showed that he had lost none of his speed and guile. A strong challenge for pole position by Senna's Ford powered McLaren made qualifying reminisent of past battles both had fought with each other. Prost eventually gained the starting advantage. The second row comprised of the young chargers Hill and Schumacher. The prospect of Prost and Senna's run to the first corner was greeted with relish, however, the Frenchman's poor start denied the crowd this spectacle. Instead it was teammate Hill who led an albeit shortlived challenge to Senna. The inexperienced Hill got too close to Senna before spinning down the field, leaving the chase to Schumacher. By lap 13 Prost had reeled in the two Ford powered cars. With Schumacher's co-operation he moved into second easily. There was no such help from Senna. Following several aborted passing manoeuvres, Prost took the lead on lap 25 and not even the torrential downpour towards the end of the race threatened his lead. After the pitstops Senna and Schumacher were still together, but Schumacher's efforts to pass the McLaren ended in tears, contact was made and the Benetton was out. Senna settled for second, his car's handling deteriorating as the race progressed. Third went to a delighted Mark Blundell, who had run competitively all weekend in the Ligier.

The underfunded Minardi team has over the years embarrassed many of its better funded rivals. The first race of the season with Ford engines and Christian Fittipaldi showed his and the cars potential. Despite mechanical problems and traffic, he proved competitive throughout practice. 15th on the grid, he made consistent progress through the field after spinning on lap 6. The balance and grip of his car enabled him to run the race distance without stopping for tyres. He comfortably fended off the advances of Herbert and Berger to finish in a fine fourth position.

"South Africa, the first race of the season, and I thought that things could go well, but not so well as they did. We only did about 2-3 days testing in February in Estoril when the car was brand new. It was a completely new chassis and engine. I was expecting more mechanical problems at Kyalami, but we did not have any. I was hoping that the points would arrive this season, but was expecting them later on. On Saturday morning in free practice everything was really good and I was sixth quickest. In qualifying on Saturday afternoon I got stuck in a lot of traffic on both sets of tyres. Luckily, on my second set I just managed to pop in a reasonably quick lap, but the tyres had already gone off. If that had not happened, I think I could have qualified even higher, top eight maybe.

The first race is always very hard physically. No matter how much testing you do, you only get race fit after 2-3 races, and until then those races are very difficult. I was well prepared physically and I did not have any major problems, so I was not really nervous as the race approached. How much mental preparation I do before the start of the race depends on my mood and how I wake up in the morning. Some days I need more concentration and need to be quiet. When I put on my helmet I get in the car and stay there, not even getting out on the grid, and I sit quietly preparing, thinking of the start.

There are some guys that I have enormous respect for in F1. A lot of them are very tough. In South Africa I had Brundle starting 12th and Barrichello starting 14th. I was sure Rubens was going to take it very easy because it was his first race, so I did not have to worry a lot about him. Brundle would be giving it everything. He was in a new team and he wanted to prove a point that even going to Ligier he was capable of doing a fantastic job.

The start was O.K. The car was O.K. It was jumping a little bit too much, the tyre wear was low and grip was very, very good. On the sixth lap I braked quite late and then, when I put more pressure on the brake pedal, the foot rest broke. Then I put extra pressure on the pedal, locked the wheels and spun. Fortunately, when I was spinning the foot rest moved under my seat, where it stayed, so it did not cause me a problem. For the next 2-3 laps it was strange to drive without a foot rest, but after that I got used to it. I could have been unlucky and, if it got stuck in the pedals, I would have had to stop.

After I spun I had to make up places and I passed both Footworks, Barbazza and the Scuderias. After about 25 laps

Herbert changed tyres. When he came out again he was right behind me and he closed the gap on the first lap. After that I began to go away from him and he did not gain any time on me, even on fresh tyres. I then realised that the car was really going well and that I was going to keep a really quick pace in the race. I was really pushing a lot and the car was working really well. About 40 or 50 laps into the race I knew that if I had not already pitted for tyres it would be very difficult for me to do so and regain my position. Before the race we talked about trying to do the full distance without changing tyres, because we had a good balance in the warm up, when we ran old tyres and the car ran really well. In the end the team asked me to decide. If I thought there was a need for tyres I was to call them on the radio, but if there was the chance of continuing, and they could see my lap times in relation to the others, I would continue on the same set. That was what I decided to do. I was P5 and Berger, who had already changed his tyres, was P6. To catch Blundell he was a lot in front of me, so I just concentrated on the difference between me and the Ferrari behind me. Berger would catch me, then I would push and open up a gap, despite running my old tyres, and this happened for the last 25 laps. In the closing stages it was a case of keeping cool and concentrating on getting the car to the finish and not letting my mind wander, thinking about a possible podium finish. It was a very positive result but this season I was expecting that little bit more.

Christian Fittipaldi

FINISHING ORDER

	DRIVER	CAR	AVERAGE	DELAY
1.	**Alain Prost**	Williams	186.403	—
2.	**Ayrton Senna**	McLaren	183.925	1'19"824
3.	**Mark Blundell**	Ligier	182.633	1 lap
4.	**Christian Fittipaldi**	Minardi	181.262	1 lap
5.	**J.J. Lehto**	Sauber	177.858	2 laps
6.	**Gerhard Berger**	Ferrari	181.821	3 laps
7.	**Derek Warwick**	Footwork	178.693	3 laps

RETIREMENTS

DRIVER	CAR	LAPS	REASON
Andrea De Cesaris	Tyrrell	0	Transmission
Ukyo Katayama	Tyrrell	1	Transmission
Ivan Capelli	Jordan	2	Accident
Michael Andretti	McLaren	4	Accident
Alessandro Zanardi	Lotus	16	Accident
Damon Hill	Williams	16	Accident
Luca Badoer	Lola Bms	20	Gear
Aguri Suzuki	Footwork	21	Accident
Fabrizio Barbazza	Minardi	21	Accident
Philippe Alliot	Larrousse	27	Went off track
Jean Alesi	Ferrari	30	Suspensions
Rubens Barrichello	Jordan	31	Gear
Karl Wendlinger	Sauber	33	Electronics
Johnny Herbert	Lotus	38	Engine
Michael Schumacher	Benetton	39	Accident
Riccardo Patrese	Benetton	46	Went off track
Erik Comas	Larrousse	51	Oil filter
Michele Alboreto	Lola Bms	55	Engine
Martin Brundle	Ligier	57	Went off track

BEST LAPS

DRIVER	LAP	TIME	AVE.
Prost	40	1'19"492	192.970
Lehto	52	1'20"113	191.475
Schumacher	35	1'20"323	190.974
Patrese	46	1'20"591	190.339
Blundell	45	1'20"732	190.006
Senna	38	1'20"755	189.952
Wendlinger	33	1'20"783	189.886
Comas	50	1'20"897	189.619
Brundle	50	1'20"978	189.429
Berger	55	1'21"118	189.102
Fittipaldi	34	1'21"790	187.549
Herbert	35	1'21"936	187.214
Alliot	22	1'22"108	186.822
Barrichello	30	1'22"292	186.405
Alesi	17	1'22"303	186.380
Warwick	55	1'22"742	185.391
Zanardi	16	1'23"314	184.118
Alboreto	40	1'23"496	183.717
Hill	7	1'23"715	183.236
Andretti	4	1'23"807	183.035
Suzuki	18	1'24"474	181.590
Barbazza	13	1'24"594	181.332
Badoer	12	1'26"074	178.214
Capelli	2	1'27"277	175.758
Katayama	1	1'43"402	148.349

▲ *Senna makes his storming start to lead the Williams pair into the first corner at Kyalami.*

▶ *Fittipaldi leads a midfield battle between Herbert, team mate Barbazza and the two Footwork Mugens of Suzuki and Warwick.*

BRAZIL
The race of:

Johnny Herbert

28 March 1993 • Circuit: Interlagos •
Lenght: 307,075 km • Organiser:
International Promotions Sc Ltda • Race
Director: Roland Bruynseraede •
Spectators: 32.000 • Weather: Friday
and Saturday cloudy, Sunday sunny and
rain

A. Prost Williams 1'15"866 (205,230)	**D. Hill** Williams 1'16"859 (202,579)
A. Senna McLaren 1'17"697 (200,394)	**M. Schumacher** Benetton 1'17"821 (200,075)
M. Andretti McLaren 1'18"635 (198,003)	**R. Patrese** Benetton 1'19"049 (196,966)
J.J. Lehto Sauber 1'19"207 (196,574)	**K. Wendlinger** Sauber 1'19"230 (196,516)
J. Alesi Ferrari 1'19"260 (196,442)	**M. Blundell** Ligier 1'19"296 (196,353)
P. Alliot Larrousse 1'19"340 (196,244)	**J. Herbert** Lotus 1'19"435 (196,009)
G. Berger Ferrari 1'19"561 (195,699)	**R. Barrichello** Jordan 1'19"593 (195,620)
A. Zanardi Lotus 1'19"804 (195,103)	**M. Brundle** Ligier 1'19"835 (195,027)
E. Comas Larrousse 1'19"868 (194,947)	**D. Warwick** Footwork 1'20"064 (194,469)
A. Suzuki Footwork 1'20"232 (194,062)	**C. Fittipaldi** Minardi 1'20"716 (192,899)
L. Badoer Lola Bms 1'20"908 (192,441)	**U. Katayama** Tyrrell 1'20"991 (192,244)
A. De Cesaris Tyrrell 1'21"224 (191,692)	**F. Barbazza** Minardi 1'21"228 (191,683)
M. Alboreto Lola Bms 1'21"488 (191,071)	

If Prost was to achieve his seventh Brazilian GP victory he would not only have to beat Senna on his home track at Interlagos, but would also have to contend with the frenzied support for the local hero. After practice things looked good for Prost, pole by almost a second from Hill, who in turn was a similar margin ahead of Senna. Prost led into the first corner, but behind him the midfield lay in chaos after a spectacular collision between Andretti and Berger. Senna's chances of satisfying his craving fans seemed to dwindle when on lap 24 he was given a 10 second stop-go penalty for overtaking while yellow flags were showing. No sooner had he returned to the field, having dropped back a position to 4th, than what had begun as spotting on lap 21 became a torrential downpour, which left cars scattered all over the circuit. Senna went back into the pits immediately for wets. Prost, however, who had built up a comfortable lead at the head of the field, stayed out longer than he should have on slicks due to a misunderstanding on the pit radio. His race hopes ended on lap 30 when he came upon a trail of debris left on the track by Fittipaldi and slithered helplessly into the Minardi. For the first time ever the safety car came onto the track and Hill led the field behind it. When the safety car finally pulled off the drivers were faced with a drying track. After changing tyres on lap 41 Hill led only briefly. To the wild delight of the home crowd Senna made a decisive lunge on the inside line and passed the Williams. The pair traded fastest laps, however Senna pulled away, leaving Hill to concentrate on keeping second place. In the last stages of the race the action was hap-pening further down the field as Herbert was first chased by Blundell, then Schumacher. After a superb dogfight between Herbert and Schumacher, Schumacher went on to take third. Meanwhile, Senna crossed the line to take one of his most memorable victories and McLaren's 100th GP victory.

Johnny Herbert made his GP debut at Brazil in 1989 when he achieved a memorable fourth place. This year, leading the rejuvenated Lotus Team, Herbert once again showed the flair which marked him out as a man to watch in 1989. Twelfth on the grid, he made a strong start and was running in ninth position before the storm. Timing his pit stop almost to perfection, he moved up to fifth behind the safety car and once the safety car had pulled over he was the first to change back to slicks and moved further up the field to third. He was caught by Schumacher, who applied intense pressure, and there followed an exciting, close-fought battle, before Herbert gave way on lap 69. He scored the team's first points of the season when he finished fourth.

"Testing during the winter had gone very well for the team and we were expecting a good start to the season. South Africa did not reach our expectations, so it was difficult afterwards and we had to do work on the car and improve it a little before Brazil. Interlagos is a power circuit, but we believed that if we could get the car right, then our engine would not be such a disadvantage. We knew that we had the potential to do quite well. I didn't qualify well, but I was happier with the car than in South Africa. On Friday morning I was sixth fastest, but on Friday afternoon an oil leak sent me spinning into the pit approach lane, where there was a fire at the back of the car. There was a marshall with a fire extinguisher, but he couldn't pull the pin out of it because the gloves on his finger were too big to go through the pin. I let him have a try and then I grabbed it and extinguished the fire.
I don't get nervous at all until about an hour before the start of the race. At Brazil I didn't have a particular race strategy, but, because I was twelfth on the grid, I knew that it was a case of making up as much ground as possible and the easiest way of doing that is in the pits. The rain came and it was a big opportunity to pick up a lot of places. When the safety car came out on the circuit, I talked to the team on the radio, which is something I don't normally do, usually because it breaks up badly and you can't hear it when going round. We thought it would be a good decision to come straight into the pits for tyres because everybody was going to have to change tyres anyway. It would have been absolutely perfect if I could have done it a couple of laps earlier, but it was hard to know when the safety car was going to pull off.
When the safety car pulled off, the adrenalin came back and I just got straight back into it. By then 3/4 of the track was dry and I gained almost a lap on most of the leaders. I

don't understand why I was the only one who did it. I remember coming out and I was not far behind Damon and Senna, so I gained a hell of a lot of time. I was third for most of the time and I was hoping to get third, but the car was just not quite quick enough. Schumacher was about two seconds a lap quicker than me. He caught me and I was hopeful that I could keep him at bay, but to be honest he squeezed when he eventually took me. I got him back, but I just could not hold him down the straight. I could've just stuck in there and maybe done a bit of wheel banging or something as he would have done. He ran wide at one point after passing me on the straight and tried to go down the outside. He was moving over on me. I could have stuck in there and closed the door on him, but it was not really worth it though. Both of us could have gone off or he might have gone off and I could have carried on, but the team needed the points and we needed to finish. It was a bit of fun and it was still a good result. If it had happened somewhere else I would not have let him go."

Johnny Herbert

FINISHING ORDER

	DRIVER	CAR	AVERAGE	DELAY
1.	**Ayrton Senna**	McLaren	165.601	—
2.	**Damon Hill**	Williams	165.190	16"625
3.	**Michael Schumacher**	Benetton	164.482	45"436
4.	**Johnny Herbert**	Lotus	164.454	46"557
5.	**Mark Blundell**	Ligier	164.318	52"127
6.	**Alessandro Zanardi**	Lotus	162.818	1 lap
7.	**Philippe Alliot**	Larrousse	162.329	1 lap
8.	**Jean Alesi**	Ferrari	162.015	1 lap
9.	**Derek Warwick**	Footwork	160.116	2 laps
10.	**Erik Comas**	Larrousse	159.937	2 laps
11.	**Michele Alboreto**	Lola Bms	158.374	3 laps
12.	**Luca Badoer**	Lola Bms	157.637	3 laps

RETIREMENTS

DRIVER	CAR	LAPS	REASON
Fabrizio Barbazza	Minardi	1	Accident
Martin Brundle	Ligier	1	Accident
Gerhard Berger	Ferrari	1	Accident
Michael Andretti	McLaren	1	Accident
Riccardo Patrese	Benetton	3	Suspension
Rubens Barrichello	Jordan	13	Gear
Ukyo Katayama	Tyrrell	26	Accident
Aguri Suzuki	Footwork	27	Accident
Christian Fittipaldi	Minardi	28	Accident
Alain Prost	Williams	29	Accident
Andrea De Cesaris	Tyrrell	48	Electronics
J.J. Lehto	Sauber	52	Electronics
Karl Wendlinger	Sauber	61	Overheating

BEST LAPS

DRIVER	LAP	TIME	AVE.
Schumacher	61	1'20"024	194.567
Senna	59	1'20"187	194.171
Hill	53	1'20"794	192.712
Blundell	56	1'21"235	191.666
Prost	24	1'21"780	190.389
Alesi	58	1'22"019	189.834
Herbert	63	1'22"503	188.720
Zanardi	70	1'22"539	188.638
Wendlinger	61	1'22"859	187.910
Warwick	60	1'23"071	187.430
Lehto	52	1'23"755	185.899
Badoer	60	1'23"774	185.857
Alliot	62	1'23"835	185.722
Comas	56	1'23"877	185.629
Fittipaldi	22	1'24"211	184.893
Alboreto	64	1'24"329	184.634
Barrichello	12	1'24"798	183.613
Suzuki	23	1'25"483	182.141
De Cesaris	48	1'26"032	180.979
Patrese	2	1'26"663	179.661
Katayama	8	1'26"914	179.143

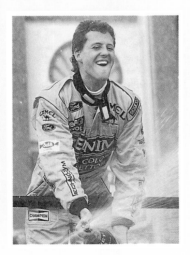

▲ *Michael Schumacher shares his delight with the partisan Brazilian crowd.*

◄ *Damon Hill leads Senna and Schumacher mid way through the race only to be passed by the unstoppable Ayrton Senna.*

► *Eddie Jordan and engine supplier Brian Hart confer in the pits.*

EUROPE

The race of:

Rubens Barrichello

11 April 1993 • Circuit: Donington • Length: 305,748 km • Organiser: Rac Msa Ltd • Race Director: Roland Bruynseraede • Spectators: 25.000 • Weather: Friday rain, Saturday clear, Sunday rain

A. Prost Williams 1'10"458 (205,552)	**D. Hill** Williams 1'10"762 (204,669)
M. Schumacher Benetton 1'12"008 (201,128)	**A. Senna** McLaren 1'12"107 (200,852)
K. Wendlinger Sauber 1'12"738 (199,109)	**M. Andretti** McLaren 1'12"739 (199,106)
J.J. Lehto Sauber 1'12"763 (199,041)	**G. Berger** Ferrari 1'12"862 (198,770)
J. Alesi Ferrari 1'12"980 (198,449)	**R. Patrese** Benetton 1'12"982 (198,443)
J. Herbert Lotus 1'13"328 (197,507)	**R. Barrichello** Jordan 1'13"514 (197,007)
A. Zanardi Lotus 1'13"560 (196,884)	**D. Warwick** Footwork 1'13"664 (196,606)
P. Alliot Larrousse 1'13"665 (196,604)	**C. Fittipaldi** Minardi 1'13"666 (196,601)
E. Comas Larrousse 1'13"970 (195,793)	**U. Katayama** Tyrrell 1'14"121 (195,394)
T. Boutsen Jordan 1'14"246 (195,065)	**F. Barbazza** Minardi 1'14"274 (194,992)
M. Blundell Ligier 1'14"301 (194,921)	**M. Brundle** Ligier 1'14"306 (194,908)
A. Suzuki Footwork 1'14"927 (193,292)	**M. Alboreto** Lola Bms 1'15"322 (192,278)
A. De Cesaris Tyrrell 1'15"417 (192,036)	

Any race organised to take place in England in early April runs the risk of being wet. Sure enough, at Donington the rain came, although it went for long enough on Saturday for Prost and Hill to show time advantage in the dry and claim the front row, with Schumacher and Senna third and fourth respectively. The pattern of the race was set in the early laps, which were dominated by two Brazilians. Having fallen back to fifth at Redgate, Senna moved through the field with an astonishing display of aggression and skill, taking the lead at the Melbourne Hairpin. Barrichello, twelfth on the grid, drove an equally startling first lap, dispatching with all but Senna, Prost and Hill. Meanwhile Andretti tangled with Wendlinger and both came off at Coppice. Intermittent rainfall made for a farcical number of pitstops and those who faired best in the ever changing conditions were those who stayed out rather than respond to each and every change. Prost came in a total of seven times! Yet another change for slicks led to disaster for Prost on lap 48 as he stalled the engine and was lapped by Senna. Having driven a fantastic race Senna came home an unchallenged first, Hill a fine second and Prost a damp third.

Every few years a new driver comes onto the scene and creates a stir with an early race performance. In 1993 that driver was Barrichello and the race was at Donington, his third GP. Impressive in qualifying, he was twelfth on the grid and gave a stunning performance in the first lap, moving up the field to fourth. From there he moved up to third, but heartbreak came on lap 71 when fuel pressure problems forced his retirement.

"Donington was almost like my home track. We had tested there before and I expected to do well. I start to mentally prepare for a race 30 minutes before I get into the car. I used to be superstitious and always got into the car on the righthand side, but I've been a long time racing and this was dropped with time. In Karts I used to wear the same underwear for every race!

The wet is a great leveller. It's more equal and there is more chance to get to the front. I love the wet conditions. I went for it and had a lucky first lap. Visibility was not as bad as it could have been. At the time of Andretti's accident I was fighting with Alesi and I only caught a glimpse of it from the corner of my eye. I tried to be as careful as possible and it was O.K. When I climbed up to fourth it was like a dream for me. I even thought on the first lap "I'm fourth now, but the Ferraris, Benetton, they will come , but I will still be sixth." If Alesi or Schumacher came to pass me, then there would be no problem. I would have been happy if I was tenth because I would have known that I had had control of the race and had been fourth, so anything could have happened and I would have been happy. When I started to go away from them and catch the Williams it was fantastic for me just to enjoy it. I could handle the situation. I wasn't on the limit pushing very hard to get in front of them and it was O.K. I was talking a lot with Gary Anderson on the radio. Some drivers do not like talking on the radio, but I don't mind. If I talk to them on the straight they cannot hear, so I talk in the corner, when I'm off the throttle, but that sometimes is not very good. Before the race we were joking because up until Donington I had not done any pit stops at all. I was joking saying "Now I'm in F1 I want to do a pit stop, please." and I did it six times! So it was unbelievable. I was laughing in the car, saying I asked for a pit stop but not six. I did not worry about doing that many stops. I was thinking "When I come in I will go back out to 8th or 10th place and I'll have to come through the field all over again" but, I was never lower than fourth place so the stops were good. Then I saw P2 on my board and I thought I was going to win the race. I could not believe it and was joking with myself because it was a situation I was not expecting. It was not long before I was lapping people. Patrese was not expecting me to lap him and I had to commit myself fully to pass him. Like me with Senna. When I saw Senna coming I thought he was second and I was first. It was a difficult race to know where people were and you came across situations you would never have expected.

On lap 48 I overtook Prost on the pitstop. It was raining heavily again and I was quicker than him. He was not going to catch me and I thought I would be on the podium. When I overtook Hill for 2nd, it was a maximum for me. I thought "Oh, my God, what am I doing here? It's a dream!" I just wanted to see my father's face. My whole life I have been trying to get into F1. Seeing my father's face seeing the positions *"Senna 1st, Barrichello 2nd"* would have been a great moment. Then six laps from the end of the race the low fuel pressure light came on. I did one more lap and the car just stopped dead. Even when I stopped I was still happy. I did everything right and I was the hero of that day. The day after the race was the worst for me. It was not fair and I just wanted to cry, because I did not get to stand next to Ayrton on the podium and hear the Brazilian anthem. I enjoyed it while I was up there and as long as I believe in myself there will be many other good times."

Rubens Barrichello

FINISHING ORDER

	DRIVER	CAR	AVERAGE	DELAY
1.	**Ayrton Senna**	McLaren	165.603	–
2.	**Damon Hill**	Williams	163.556	1'23"199
3.	**Alain Prost**	Williams	162.780	1 lap
4.	**Johnny Herbert**	Lotus	160.972	1 lap
5.	**Riccardo Patrese**	Benetton	160.171	2 laps
6.	**Fabrizio Barbazza**	Minardi	159.881	2 laps
7.	**Christian Fittipaldi**	Minardi	158.880	3 laps
8.	**Alessandro Zanardi**	Lotus	156.802	4 laps
9.	**Erik Comas**	Larrousse	154.857	4 laps
10.	**Rubens Barrichello**	Jordan	163.418	6 laps
11.	**Michele Alboreto**	Lola Bms	151.692	6 laps

RETIREMENTS

DRIVER	CAR	LAPS	REASON
Michael Andretti	McLaren	1	Accident
Karl Wendlinger	Sauber	1	Accident
Martin Brundle	Ligier	7	About face
Ukyo Katayama	Tyrrell	11	Clutch
J.J. Lehto	Sauber	13	Whitdrawn
Gerhard Berger	Ferrari	19	Suspension
Mark Blundell	Ligier	20	Went off track
Michael Schumacher	Benetton	22	About face
Philippe Alliot	Larrousse	27	Accident
Aguri Suzuki	Footwork	29	Went off track
Jean Alesi	Ferrari	36	Suspension
Andrea De Cesaris	Tyrrell	55	Gear
Thierry Boutsen	Jordan	61	Accelerator
Derek Warwick	Footwork	66	Gear

BEST LAPS

DRIVER	LAP	TIME	AVE.
Senna	57	1'18"029	185.608
Hill	55	1'19"379	182.451
Prost	55	1'19"756	181.589
Zanardi	51	1'20"801	179.240
Fittipaldi	52	1'21"022	178.751
Warwick	54	1'22"061	176.488
Herbert	55	1'22"150	176.297
Comas	52	1'22"200	176.190
Patrese	54	1'22"279	176.021
Barrichello	55	1'22"307	175.961
Schumacher	21	1'22"549	175.445
Alesi	21	1'22"550	175.443
Blundell	20	1'24"093	172.224
Barbazza	21	1'24"703	170.983
Alliot	19	1'25"078	170.230
Boutsen	19	1'25"532	169.326
Berger	17	1'26"078	168.252
De Cesaris	51	1'26"419	167.588
Alboreto	19	1'28"023	164.534
Suzuki	20	1'28"929	162.858
Brundle	5	1'33"123	155.523
Katayama	5	1'33"528	154.850
Lehto	2	1'37"749	148.163

▶ *The cars funnel through into Craner Curves on the first lap at Donington.*

▼ *Senna and Hill on their way to 1st and 2nd in the Sega European Grand Prix.*

▼▶ *Rubens Barrichello leads Alain Prost in only his third Grand Prix.*

SAN MARINO
The race of:

J.J. Lehto

25 April 1993 • Circuit: Enzo e Dino Ferrari • Length: 307,440 km • Organiser: Sagis • Race Director: Roland Bruynseraede • Spectators: 70.000 • Weather: Friday and Saturday clear, Sunday rain

A. Prost Williams 1'22"070 (221,080)	**D. Hill** Williams 1'22"168 (220,816)
M. Schumacher Benetton 1'23"919 (216,208)	**A. Senna** McLaren 1'24"007 (215,982)
K. Wendlinger Sauber 1'24"720 (214,164)	**M. Andretti** McLaren 1'24"793 (213,980)
M. Blundell Ligier 1'24"804 (213,952)	**G. Berger** Ferrari 1'24"822 (213,907)
J. Alesi Ferrari 1'24"829 (213,889)	**M. Brundle** Ligier 1'24"893 (213,728)
R. Patrese Benetton 1'24"896 (213,720)	**J. Herbert** Lotus 1'25"115 (213,170)
R. Barrichello Jordan 1'25"169 (213,035)	**P. Alliot** Larrousse 1'25"482 (212,255)
D. Warwick Footwork 1'25"901 (211,220)	**J.J. Lehto** Sauber 1'25"941 (211,122)
E. Comas Larrousse 1'26"279 (210,295)	**A. De Cesaris** Tyrrell 1'26"429 (209,930)
T. Boutsen Jordan 1'26"436 (209,913)	**A. Zanardi** Lotus 1'26"465 (209,842)
A. Suzuki Footwork 1'26"657 (209,377)	**U. Katayama** Tyrrell 1'26"900 (208,792)
C. Fittipaldi Minardi 1'27"277 (207,890)	**L. Badoer** Lola Bms 1'27"371 (207,666)
F. Barbazza Minardi 1'27"602 (207,119)	

After the disappointments of rain-affected Interlagos and Donington Alain Prost needed to re-establish his dominance at Imola. It began to rain two hours before the start, but Prost's determination to overcome the conditions was evidenced when he was fastest by a clear second during extra practice to acclimatise to the wet conditions. Although the rain had stopped, the race was declared wet. Prost suffered a slight clutch problem during the warm up and made a poor start, ending the first lap third behind teammate Hill and Senna, with Schumacher, Berger, and Wendlinger completing the top six. With a daring manoeuvre Prost passed Senna on the long drag out of Tosa on the wet line on lap seven, however, what was bravely gained was swiftly lost. After a lengthy pit stop for dry tyres Prost found himself once again behind Senna, who in turn was right on Hill's tail. On the twelfth lap Prost repeated his audacious manoeuvre on Senna exiting Tosa, and in the same swoop also passed his teammate for the lead. The Frenchman drove unchallenged to the flag, not even letting a sticking throttle affect his dominance of the race. Hill's race ended in the sandtrap, caught out by a "long" brake pedal. On lap 43 Senna's McLaren suffered hydraulic failure, costing him a secure second and six valuable points. These finally went to Schumacher, with Brundle third, scoring another excellent result for Ligier.

J.J. Lehto's fourth position at Imola was a tribute to the competitiveness of the new Sauber in it's first year of Grand Prix racing and to his tenacious driving in a car that was on full wet settings and with a failing engine. After a disappointing practice JJ made a great start. He gained further places with a well timed pitstop and successfully battled with both Lotuses and teammate Karl Wendlinger. When trying to nurse his ailing car to the finish in the closing stages the engine blew on the last lap, but he was still classified fourth.

"We were testing all winter and were ready at the beginning of the season. That was a big advantage, so the first races were very good for us. Imola has always been a good circuit for me, and it's where I scored my first podium finish in 1991, so I went there with high hopes. We had a number of problems in practice. We had to change a lot of things at this circuit. The track changes from downhill to uphill, slow corners, quick corners, chicanes. You have to compromise in set up between downforce in the corners and speed in a straight line. Also for some reason, when the weather is cool the car is quicker than in hot weather. We don't know why, and luckily it was not hot over the weekend.

Basically, I prepare for the race all weekend! Saturday evening I will start to think about the race in bed and drive the course in my mind. Then after the driver briefing and presentation there is one hour when I like to be alone, not think of anything else, just prepare for the race. As for superstitions, I always get into and out of the car from the left hand side.

Practice was dry, but at the beginning the race was wet. For me this was not a problem. I like driving in the rain and the wet conditions are good to me always. I'm always prepared for the rain and sometimes I hope for it, like Senna does. Even if it had stayed wet throughout, I think the result would have been more or less the same. Being in the top three with a normal car is difficult at the moment. Even if you are quick and the car is running very well, you still need a little bit of luck.

At the beginning of the race the most important thing is to get through the first corner. There are always some drivers you know are trickier than others. Sometimes they try some funny business, but every start is a little bit different. You never know what will happen. I wanted to see what the others were doing and let the race settle down and not be too severe on the tyres. I was able to pick off a number of people without any problems. I saw Blundell bouncing off the lefthand side of the wall at Tamburello. I was not involved. I had to brake a little and visibility was bad because of the spray and dirt.

I made the decision to come in for tyres myself. I hate talking to the pit on the radio. At some circuits the frequencies are very close so you hear the other teams and that is a pain in the arse, especially in the middle of the corner when you concentration needs to be total. If somebody tries to talk to me during a lap, it does affect my driving.

By lap 41 I was caught up in a fight with the Lotuses and with Karl. When Karl was in front of me I was quicker than he was, but it was hard to pass because there was only one dry line. It was a very competitive race, with a lot of cars evenly matched, especially the Lotuses, Johnny and Zanardi. I fought with the Lotuses like hell and had to concentrate really hard. Eventually Zanardi made a mistake. He was braking too hard, lost the rear and spun. Johnny blew the engine, which is what happened to me on the last lap, but luckily I was ahead of Alliot, so still kept the position.

All the race I had the red warning light showing. The oil pressure was going down. In the end the sump was dry and it blew. I was praying "Please hold together". The performance was dying off all the time. I had to be careful in the corners not to push hard, because the G forces were taking the oil out of the sump. On the last lap I was telling myself "No hurry. Slow down", but then it blew up by the paddock. I was so angry. I had worked so hard and everything had held together so well. I had a lift back to the paddock with Alliot and neither of us knew who was fourth. He said "Well done, you're fourth", but I said "No, it's you". Then people came up congratulating me. I was delighted as it was only the fourth race of the season and it was my second lot of points."

J.J. Lehto

FINISHING ORDER

	DRIVER	CAR	AVERAGE	DELAY
1.	**Alain Prost**	Williams	197.625	–
2.	**Michael Schumacher**	Benetton	196.488	32"410
3.	**Mark Blundell**	Ligier	193.681	1 lap
4.	**J.J. Lehto**	Sauber	193.568	2 laps
5.	**Philippe Alliot**	Larrousse	190.323	2 laps
6.	**Fabrizio Barbazza**	Minardi	189.244	2 laps
7.	**Luca Badoer**	Lola Bms	185.025	3 laps
8.	**Johnny Herbert**	Lotus	193.421	4 laps
9.	**Aguri Suzuki**	Footwork	173.505	7 laps

RETIREMENTS

DRIVER	CAR	LAPS	REASON
Riccardo Patrese	Benetton	1	About face
Mark Blundell	Ligier	1	Accident
Thierry Boutsen	Jordan	1	Gear
Gerhard Berger	Ferrari	8	Gear
Rubens Barrichello	Jordan	17	About face
Andrea De Cesaris	Tyrrell	18	Gear
Erik Comas	Larrousse	18	Oil pressure
Damon Hill	Williams	20	Went off track
Ukyo Katayama	Tyrrell	22	Overheating
Derek Warwick	Footwork	29	Went off track
Michael Andretti	McLaren	32	Went off track
Christian Fittipaldi	Minardi	36	Trim
Jean Alesi	Ferrari	40	Clutch
Ayrton Senna	McLaren	42	Suspension
Karl Wendlinger	Sauber	48	Engine
Alessandro Zanardi	Lotus	53	Went off track

BEST LAPS

DRIVER	LAP	TIME	AVE.
Prost	42	1'26"128	210.663
Schumacher	41	1'26"612	209.486
Senna	28	1'27"490	207.384
Zanardi	41	1'27"690	206.911
Alesi	30	1'28"317	205.442
Herbert	45	1'28"324	205.425
Brundle	45	1'28"430	205.179
Hill	19	1'28"590	204.809
Alliot	48	1'26"636	204.702
Andretti	30	1'28"803	204.317
Warwick	28	1'28"874	204.154
Lehto	44	1'29"092	203.655
Wendlinger	30	1'29"304	203.171
Suzuki	29	1'29"332	203.108
Barbazza	39	1'29"646	202.396
Fittipaldi	22	1'30"438	200.624
Comas	15	1'30"983	199.422
Badoer	46	1'31"751	197.753
Barrichello	15	1'32"432	196.296
Katayama	19	1'33"541	193.968
De Cesaris	18	1'34"556	191.886
Berger	8	1'42"881	176.359
Boutsen	1	12'17"162	24.613

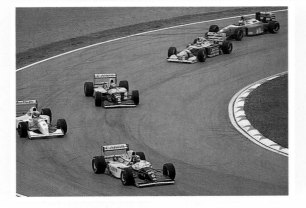

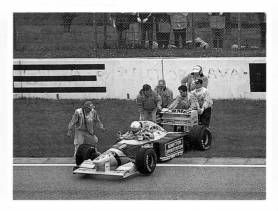

▲ **The leaders scrabble for grip at Tosa on the slippery surface.**

▲▶ **Patrese didn't find any grip at Tosa and his dissapointing season continued.**

▶ **JJ Lehto and Peter Sauber confer over settings for the changeable conditions of the San Marino Grand Prix.**

SPAIN
The race of:

Michael Andretti

9 May 1993 • Circuit: Barcellona • Length: 308,555 km • Organiser: Real Automobil Club de Catalunya • Race Director: Roland Bruynseraede • Spectators: 40.000 • Weather: sunny all three days

A. Prost Williams 1'17"809 (219,630)	**D. Hill** Williams 1'18"346 (218,125)
A. Senna McLaren 1'19"722 (214,360)	**M. Schumacher** Benetton 1'20"520 (212,235)
R. Patrese Benetton 1'20"600 (212,025)	**K. Wendlinger** Sauber 1'21"203 (210,450)
M. Andretti McLaren 1'21"360 (210,044)	**J. Alesi** Ferrari 1'21"767 (208,999)
J.J. Lehto Sauber 1'22"047 (208,285)	**J. Herbert** Lotus 1'22"470 (207,217)
G. Berger Ferrari 1'22"655 (206,753)	**M. Blundell** Ligier 1'22"708 (206,621)
P. Alliot Larrousse 1'22"887 (206,175)	**E. Comas** Larrousse 1'22"904 (206,132)
A. Zanardi Lotus 1'23"026 (205,829)	**D. Warwick** Footwork 1'23"086 (205,681)
R. Barrichello Jordan 1'23"232 (205,320)	**M. Brundle** Ligier 1'23"357 (205,012)
A. Suzuki Footwork 1'23"432 (204,828)	**C. Fittipaldi** Minardi 1'23"449 (204,786)
T. Boutsen Jordan 1'23"464 (204,749)	**L. Badoer** Lola Bms 1'24"268 (202,796)
U. Katayama Tyrrell 1'24"291 (202,741)	**A. De Cesaris** Tyrrell 1'24"358 (202,579)
F. Barbazza Minardi 1'24"399 (202,481)	

At Barcelona the dominance of Williams-Renault was complete. In practice nobody came close to posing a threat. Almost two seconds separated pole-sitter Prost from Senna, the nearest challenger and perhaps Senna's hopes evaporated when the rain that was forecast for the race day never arrived. On the run to the first corner Hill got the better of Prost, as Prost was distracted by Senna's advances. On lap 11 Prost passed Hill for the lead, but his hard work in opening a three second gap was undone when he was delayed whilst laping Warwick. By lap 22 both Williams were together again and Prost could not pull away. He later complained of deteriorating handling. Hill sat menacingly behind his teammate, looking entirely at ease and waiting for a mistake. Disaster struck for Hill when his engine blew without warning on lap 41. Senna and Schumacher fought for third and honours in the Ford battle. Both were held up by backmarkers and a slippery track caused by the oil from the high number of engine failures. Senna came in for tyres late in the race on lap 52 and a lengthy pitstop of 15 seconds allowed Schumacher to close right up and challenge for second following a series of fastest laps. Schumacher was forced to settle for third after he recovered from being sent into the gravel following the blow up of Zanardi's engine.

Perhaps it is no coincidence that the nightmare that Michael Andretti's debut season in F1 had become ended at Barcelona. It was the first track that he had previously visited and he looked comfortable throughout practice. He was sixth after the first qualifying session before dropping to seventh on the grid. Determined to bring his car home, he drove a steady and consistent race, showing great restraint throughout. Despite handling difficulties he ran sixth in the race until Hill's retirement and collected his first Championship points.

"Going to Spain I definitely felt that the pressure was on me to finish a race. I approached Barcelona differently. I was determined to drive to the finish, so in the end it was just the race I wanted. I drove at seven-tenths and was just thinking "Bring it home, don't make a mistake". I was trying to be careful to finish. It was not my natural style of racing and I did not enjoy the race, but I achieved my goal.

I think that my grid position was good. I was fourth in the first practice and that was pretty good. The only problem was that the car was probably at its worst on that weekend. The handling seemed to get worse as the weekend went on. The car did not have any backend, it kept on jumping on me through the fast corners. That made it very difficult and it was unfortunate.

I was happy to drive alongside Ayrton Senna and to be compared with the best driver in the world. One of the advantages was that I was learning a lot from Ayrton. He helped me a lot. The downside is that he is so quick and that makes your job really tough. He was carrying a bad car. I believe that when the car was not very good he would have been getting the same results in qualifying if he had been in a Lotus. He would be the first to tell you that it was the worst car he had ever driven. However, he was able to carry it and on occasions he made me look pretty bad.

I'm always tuned in for a race, but the closer it gets the more tuned in I feel. I don't do any one thing to prepare, it's a natural process. During the early races of the season it didn't help me not knowing the reputations of the other drivers. You always do have mental notes on different drivers and my notes were pretty slim.

I had problems adapting to standing starts for sure, because I had never done them before. Having traction control actually made it more difficult and it did not help that the engine died on me on occasions. They are difficult and if you've not done them it is that much more difficult.

The start at Barcelona was really strange. The lights went to yellow instead of green. Some guys were hesitating a bit and I was looking for yellow flags, but didn't see any. Everybody stood on it, then backed off, then stood on it again. At turn one everybody was a little tentative. We did not know what was going on.

I think I could have passed Patrese on turn one, but I resisted the temptation and decided to be careful. It's a shame, because I think that if I had got him, he would have had a tough time getting by me. I was being careful in traffic. Then I was just waiting for something to go wrong. What made it a good race for me to finish was that I was going by myself the whole race. I did not have any pressure from the back and I was not catching anybody at the front. I ran at my own pace throughout and in terms of getting race miles it was very good for me.

In some ways Indycar is similar to F1 and in other ways it is not. Having a race strategy is important in both. In F1 you don't have to make pitstops. You can go into a race not knowing if you're going to make a pitstop and you have to play it by ear and monitor the situation on the radio. On the other hand, in Indycars you have yellow flags, you know that you've got to stop for fuel. So strategy is a little different. Still, staying in communication by radio is important. I know that some guys talk all of the time, but I don't like to talk on the radio and so talk a bare minimum, but keep communication up.

It was a strange race, but not very satisfying. It was satisfying because I finished the race and got my first points, but I did not feel good after the race, because I was driving to finish rather than racing in my natural style."

Michael Andretti

FINISHING ORDER

	DRIVER	CAR	AVERAGE	DELAY
1.	**Alain Prost**	Williams	200.227	–
2.	**Ayrton Senna**	McLaren	199.620	16.873
3.	**Michael Schumacher**	Benetton	199.253	27.125
4.	**Riccardo Patrese**	Benetton	197.026	1 lap
5.	**Michael Andretti**	McLaren	195.814	1 lap
6.	**Gerhard Berger**	Ferrari	193.282	2 laps
7.	**Mark Blundell**	Ligier	192.982	2 laps
8.	**Christian Fittipaldi**	Minardi	192.601	2 laps
9.	**Erik Comas**	Larrousse	192.118	2 laps
10.	**Aguri Suzuki**	Footwork	191.020	2 laps
11.	**Thierry Boutsen**	Jordan	190.621	3 laps
12.	**Rubens Barrichello**	Jordan	190.531	3 laps
13.	**Derek Warwick**	Footwork	190.521	3 laps
14.	**Alessandro Zanardi**	Lotus	193.007	5 laps

RETIREMENTS

DRIVER	CAR	LAPS	REASON
Johnny Herbert	Lotus	2	Suspension
Ukyo Katayama	Tyrrell	11	About-face
Martin Brundle	Ligier	11	Wheel
Philippe Alliot	Larrousse	26	Differential
Fabrizio Barbazza	Minardi	37	About-face
Jean Alesi	Ferrari	40	Engine
Damon Hill	Williams	41	Engine
Andrea De Cesaris	Tyrrell	42	Disqualified
Karl Wendlinger	Sauber	42	Fuel pressure
Luca Badoer	Lola Bms	43	Gear
J.J. Lehto	Sauber	53	Engine

BEST LAPS

DRIVER	LAP	TIME	AVE.
Schumacher	61	1'20"989	211.006
Senna	61	1'21"717	209.127
Hill	40	1'22"840	206.292
Prost	38	1'22"923	206.085
Andretti	59	1'23"791	203.950
Barrichello	54	1'24"085	203.237
Patrese	33	1'24"785	201.559
Wendlinger	36	1'24"933	201.208
Berger	51	1'25"065	200.896
Zanardi	59	1'25"246	200.469
Blundell	58	1'25"543	199.773
Alesi	39	1'25"729	199.340
Warwick	59	1'25"795	199.186
Fittipaldi	55	1'25"816	199.138
Boutsen	48	1'25"824	199.119
Lehto	47	1'25"824	199.119
Comas	49	1'26"381	197.835
Suzuki	58	1'27"006	196.414
De Cesaris	42	1'27"268	195.824
Alliot	23	1'27"453	195.410
Barbazza	33	1'27"899	194.419
Badoer	41	1'28"633	192.809
Katayama	11	1'29"569	190.794
Brundle	7	1'29"805	190.292
Herbert	2	1'38"480	173.530

▲ *Senna carves his way through the field in his valliant chase of race winner Prost.*

▶ *Senna and Schumacher celebrate their second and third places by spraying the very best Moet.*

▶▶ *Andretti's best result and first points of the year brought a hint of a smile to the likeable American.*

MONACO

The race of:

Ayrton Senna

23 Maj 1993 • Circuit: Montecarlo • Length: 259,584 km • Organiser: Ac Montecarlo • Race Director: Roland Bruynseraede • Spectators: 70.000 • Weather: Thursday rain, Saturday and Sunday clear

A. Prost Williams 1'20"557 (148,725)	**M. Schumacher** Benetton 1'21"190 (147,565)
A. Senna McLaren 1'21"552 (146,910)	**D. Hill** Williams 1'21"825 (146,420)
J. Alesi Ferrari 1'21"948 (146,200)	**R. Patrese** Benetton 1'22"117 (145,899)
G. Berger Ferrari 1'22"394 (145,409)	**K. Wendlinger** Sauber 1'22"477 (145,262)
M. Andretti McLaren 1'22"994 (144,357)	**E. Comas** Larrousse 1'23"246 (143,920)
J.J. Lehto Sauber 1'23"715 (143,114)	**D. Warwick** Footwork 1'23"749 (143,056)
M. Brundle Ligier 1'23"786 (142,993)	**J. Herbert** Lotus 1'23"812 (142,949)
P. Alliot Larrousse 1'23"907 (142,787)	**R. Barrichello** Jordan 1'24"086 (142,483)
C. Fittipaldi Minardi 1'24"298 (142,124)	**A. Suzuki** Footwork 1'24"524 (141,744)
A. De Cesaris Tyrrell 1'24"544 (141,711)	**A. Zanardi** Lotus 1'24"888 (141,137)
M. Blundell Ligier 1'24"972 (140,997)	**U. Katayama** Tyrrell 1'25"236 (140,560)
T. Boutsen Jordan 1'25"267 (140,509)	**M. Alboreto** Lola Bms 1'26"444 (138,596)
F. Barbazza Minardi 1'26"582 (138,375)	

It says much for Senna and Prost's domination of F1 over the last decade that one has to go back ten years to find a winner other than these two at Monaco. Grid positions at the tortuous circuit are vital and after the wet Thursday practice much rested on Saturday's final qualifying session. Prost immediately threw down the gauntlet with a time that would not be beaten all weekend. Senna's efforts to match Prost saw him hit the barriers and use the escape road. Schumacher, delighted with his car's new traction control, shared the front row with Prost. Senna settled for third and Hill, fastest after Thursday's first timed session, fourth. The field got away cleanly in grid order, but on lap 6 it was announced that Prost had been given a stop-go penalty for jumping the start. Having served the penalty Prost then stalled twice before rejoining in 22nd, a lap down. He carved his way up the field to fourth position, but still a lap down on the leaders. By lap 31 Schumacher held a 15 second lead over Senna, but two laps later the Brazilian came through first, the Benetton having retired with hydraulic failure. On lap 51 Senna, comfortably ahead of Hill, came in for tyres. By the time he rejoined the field the gap was reduced to five seconds. On fresh tyres the gap was opened once more and Senna went on to take his sixth victory at Monaco. After a narrow escape at the hairpin where he was assaulted by Berger, Hill finished a delighted second. Berger had a highly eventful race fighting with Alesi for the final podium position. Having passed his teammate he retired on the spot after his run in with Hill and handed third back to Alesi.

Ayrton Senna's amazing record at Monaco began in 1987 and since 1989 he has won each race consecutively. His victory this year broke Graham Hill's record of five wins at Monaco. Senna had an eventful weekend with more off course excursions than one would expect of the triple World Champion. He sustained an injury to his left hand, which was to trouble him for the remainder of the weekend, in an accident at Ste Devote during Thursday's free practice session. He had completed only six laps before the accident and yet he was still fastest overall. Another off at the same location on Saturday morning was followed by a third, which resulted in the loss of the McLaren's nose, as Senna strived to improve on third position on the grid. He ran a comfortable third in the race and inherited the lead after Prost's penalty and Schumacher's retirement.

"Monaco is a very special place for me. I have had so many different and intense experiences there. There was that second place in '84 - it was raining and Jacky Ickx stopped the race when I was about to overtake Prost. It was my first podium. Then there was that accident in '88, which might appear to have been a disaster, but, actually, it changed me completely for the better as a driver and as a man. Not to mention my five pole positions and now my six victories. The Grand Prix at Monaco is, without a shadow of doubt, the most important race in terms of driver challenge.

Concentration has to be at its optimum all the time, because you drive between two fences all the way through. There is no room for hesitation or error. For the spectators, I believe it is the most interesting race as as well. They can watch the race from a 2-3 meters distance and, therefore, feel for themselves what a Formula 1 race car is about - its power, noise and aggressiveness.

The accident at Ste Devote during practice was due to a problem the team has had since the beginning of the year and is related to the computer software. Afterwards I was very shaken, but conscious. It was a very hard impact. I hit a bump as I braked. The rear got away. I was lucky because the impacts were terrible, but the monocoque is strong and well built. I hit my chin in the helmet! Imagine, the helmet shook so hard with the impact that it actually moved on my head! I thought my chance in the Grand Prix had gone. I had hurt my left hand and, considering that I am left handed, it worried me a lot at the time. The difference between 99% and flat out at Monaco is a big difference. Still, I thought positively about the race, about the ways I could put some pressure on Prost and Schumacher, even if maybe I couldn't cope with them on speed. And you know, I always expect a wild card. Fortunately, we have that extra days rest in Monaco as there is no practice on Friday. I underwent a non-stop treatment and the recovery was amazing. On Saturday, it was still hurting, but I could move around and hold the steering wheel properly. So, at the beginning I thought I would not race on Sunday, because the pain was really strong, but everything went really well. I had not planned to stop for tyres, but I changed my tactics when Schumacher retired with hydraulic failure. I was not in a position to challenge Schumacher. It was the first time I had run behind the German and could immediately notice how much more power the Benetton Ford had. From then on, it was a matter of keeping a good rhythm in order not to let the gap increase too much. When Schumacher retired I started to think about people behind me and my tyre's wear. I knew I would have problems with it on the last 20 laps, so I kept pushing my pace to open a gap big enough to enable me to go into the pits without losing the lead. And that's what I did. There was a problem with the front jack and they had to change it, but I didn't lose much time. After rejoining with a five second lead, all I thought about was keeping my concentration. I know you can lose it here, that's how I lost the race in '88.

I had my first podium here with Toleman and I've won with a Lotus-Honda, V10 and V12 powered McLarens and now with a McLaren-Ford. I want to say a sincere thanks to everyone who has helped make it happen."

Ayrton Senna

FINISHING ORDER

	DRIVER	CAR	AVERAGE	DELAY
1.	**Ayrton Senna**	McLaren	138.837	–
2.	**Damon Hill**	Williams	137.770	52.118
3.	**Jean Alesi**	Ferrari	137.542	1'03.362
4.	**Alain Prost**	Williams	137.003	1 lap
5.	**Christian Fittipaldi**	Minardi	134.888	2 laps
6.	**Mark Blundell**	Ligier	134.883	2 laps
7.	**Alessandro Zanardi**	Lotus	134.322	2 laps
8.	**Michael Andretti**	McLaren	133.899	2 laps
9.	**Rubens Barrichello**	Jordan	133.679	2 laps
10.	**Andrea De Cesaris**	Tyrrell	133.664	2 laps
11.	**Fabrizio Barbazza**	Minardi	132.159	3 laps
12.	**Philippe Alliot**	Larrousse	132.140	3 laps
13.	**Karl Wendlinger**	Sauber	131.395	4 laps
14.	**Gerhard Berger**	Ferrari	138.331	8 laps

RETIREMENTS

DRIVER	CAR	LAPS	REASON
Mark Blundell	Ligier	3	Suspension
Thierry Boutsen	Jordan	12	Suspension
J.J. Lehto	Sauber	23	Accident
Michele Alboreto	Lola Bms	28	Gear
Ukyo Katayama	Tyrrell	31	Engine
Michael Schumacher	Benetton	32	Suspension
Derek Warwick	Footwork	43	Engine
Aguri Suzuki	Footwork	46	Went off track
Erik Comas	Larrousse	51	Accident
Riccardo Patrese	Benetton	53	Engine
Johnny Herbert	Lotus	61	Went off track

BEST LAPS

DRIVER	LAP	TIME	AVE.
Prost	52	1'23"604	143.304
Berger	60	1'23"660	143.208
Senna	59	1'23"737	143.077
Schumacher	18	1'24"177	142.329
Hill	52	1'24"590	141.634
Wendlinger	43	1'24"947	141.039
Brundle	69	1'25"006	140.941
Alesi	52	1'25"007	140.939
Andretti	55	1'25"102	140.782
Patrese	25	1'25"724	139.760
Zanardi	38	1'26"317	138.800
Fittipaldi	59	1'26"500	138.506
Lehto	15	1'26"559	138.412
Barrichello	75	1'26"711	138.169
Comas	17	1'26"960	137.774
Alliot	67	1'27"068	137.603
De Cesaris	65	1'27"222	137.360
Warwick	19	1'27"283	137.264
Suzuki	35	1'27"388	137.099
Herbert	21	1'27"480	136.955
Barbazza	63	1'28"235	135.783
Blundell	3	1'28"653	135.143
Boutsen	12	1'29"117	134.439
Katayama	21	1'29"315	134.141
Alboreto	11	1'29"377	134.048

▶ *Ayrton Senna celebrates with Ron Dennis a truly successful partnership in Formula One Racing.*

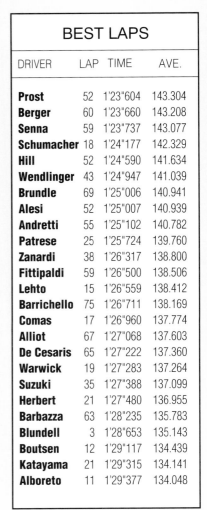

▼ *Schumacher leads Senna into Mirabeau during the early laps of the Monaco Grand Prix.*

CANADA
Tha race of:

Gerhard Berger

13 June 1993 • Circuit: Gilles Villeneuve • Length: 305,670 Km • Organiser: Ans Canada • Race Director: Roland Bruynseraede • Spectators: 70.520 • Weather: sunny all three days

A. Prost Williams 1'18"987 (201,907)		**D. Hill** Williams 1'19"491 (200,626)	
M. Schumacher Benetton 1'20"808 (197,357)		**R. Patrese** Benetton 1'20"948 (197,015)	
G. Berger Ferrari 1'21"278 (196,215)		**J. Alesi** Ferrari 1'21"414 (195,888)	
M. Brundle Ligier 1'21"603 (195,434)		**A. Senna** McLaren 1'21"706 (195,188)	
K. Wendlinger Sauber 1'21"813 (194,932)		**M. Blundell** Ligier 1'22"097 (194,258)	
J.J. Lehto Sauber 1'22"198 (194,019)		**M. Andretti** McLaren 1'22"229 (193,946)	
E. Comas Larrousse 1'22"263 (193,866)		**R. Barrichello** Jordan 1'22"509 (193,288)	
P. Alliot Larrousse 1'22"819 (192,565)		**A. Suzuki** Footwork 1'22"891 (192,397)	
C. Fittipaldi Minardi 1'23"119 (191,869)		**D. Warwick** Footwork 1'23"185 (191,717)	
A. De Cesaris Tyrrell 1'23"185 (191,715)		**J. Herbert** Lotus 1'23"223 (191,630)	
A. Zanardi Lotus 1'23"240 (191,591)		**U. Katayama** Tyrrell 1'23"824 (190,256)	
F. Barbazza Minardi 1'23"946 (189,979)		**T. Boutsen** Jordan 1'23"960 (189,948)	
L. Badoer Lola Bms 1'24"357 (189,054)			

When the teams arrived at Montreal they were greeted by a bombshell. The stewards received a report from Charlie Whiting, FISA F1 Technical Delegate, declaring that all cars using active suspension and traction control contravened the F1 technical regulations and, as such, were illegal. Several team managers pointed out that it would not be possible to convert their "active" chassis to "passive" and that if the ban was to take effect immediately they would have no alternative but to withdraw. Any decision regarding the legality of the cars must be sanctioned by the World Council and the teams were hopeful that the Council would allow them to keep the cars unchanged at least until the end of the season. The controversy centred on Article 1.3, 2.4 and 3.7 of the 1993 technical regulations. In Whiting's report it was stated that teams using traction control did so in contravention of Articles 1.3 and 2.4, in that the propulsion of the car is not under the direct control of the driver at all times. Article 3.7 makes it clear that aerodynamic devices must remain immobile in relation to the sprung part of the car. Whiting's report stated that the Williams, McLaren, Benetton, Ferrari, Tyrell, Lotus and Minardi - in short all of the teams save five -fell foul of the regulations, in that the hydraulic actuators effect the aerodynamics and do not remain immobile in relation to the chassis. After the furore had died down, the general consensus amongst team officials was that FISA had fired a warning shot across the teams' bows regarding regulations for 1994.

Prost arrived at Canada under considerable pressure following the controversy over the stewards penalty for his jump start at Monaco. He also tailed Senna in the Championship. However, Prost withstood the pressure during practice and demolished all opposition, bar teammate Hill. Schumacher led the second row of the grid almost a full two seconds slower than Prost and effectively in another race altogether. Patrese joined Schumacher to make it an all Benetton second row, having given his best qualifying performance to date for his new team. Grid positions amongst the front runners were settled on Friday, with few improving their times on Saturday owing to the deterioration in the weather conditions. Prost, perhaps haunted by the memory of Monaco, was beaten to the first corner by Hill. Schumacher got away badly and fell back to seventh due to poorly adjusted traction control. The highlight of the early laps was the progress made by Senna. After his worst qualifying performance in over five years, he started eighth. After two laps only the Williams-Renault were ahead of him. Prost took the lead on lap 6 and immediately opened up a gap with a series of fastest laps. By lap 20 he had a lead of eight seconds and Senna had caught Hill. On lap 30 Hill pitted for tyres and, after a chaotic stop, exited 17 seconds later, having fallen behind Senna and Schumacher, who had carved his way up the field with a number of audacious passes. Prost stayed out until lap 34 and changed tyres only as a precaution. With six laps to go Senna and Schumacher were as one, but the crowd were denied a battle to the flag when the McLaren's altenator broke. Prost took the flag 15 seconds clear of Schumacher after an emphatic performance that regained him the lead in the Championship and would have worried his rivals. Hill took third owing to his disasterous pitstop.

Gerhard Berger's hard earned fourth place was a tribute to the intensive development programme that Ferrari had undertaken all season. The TT spec V12 engine was available for the first time and Berger used it to qualify in fifth position. This was all the more impressive due to the time he lost in free practice on Friday as a result of a jammed gearbox and of being stranded on the circuit when his car broke down. A superb start saw Berger third on the first lap, but he let Senna, Schumacher and Alesi through in order to prolong the life of his failing brakes. For the remainder of the race he fought with the Ligier of Martin Brundle, but, despite fears over his car's excessive fuel consumption towards the end of the race, Berger kept ahead of the Briton to the flag.

"The Canadian GP, the Gilles Villeneuve Circuit and the city of Montreal all feature high up on my list of favourite races, tracks and cities.
Having won the race in 1992, I was keen to put on a good performance this year. Obviously Ferrari had been very much off the pace for the first part of the season, but both myself and Jean were encouraged by our performance in Monaco, three weeks earlier. Monaco is always considered as the first turning point in the season, so I arrived in Canada full of confi-

dence. Practice did not get off to a good start for me as I had a gearbox problem on Friday morning which caused the session to be red-flagged. All the same, fifth place was not bad, but I think it owed more to my driving than to the car.

The TT engine was used for the first time. Basically, the engine was the same as the one used previously except that it has variable length inlet trumpets that vary their height according to revs. It was a system first tried by Honda and then Renault.

I do not have any particular race strategy. It is impossible to predict what will happen after the green light. Like all the other drivers I try and make a really good start. I was penalised for doing this once in Canada. The Ferrari engine has always been particularly easy to use at the start, one of the advantages of a 12 cylinder engine. I always know which drivers are around me at the start, but this year's Canda race did not throw up a particularly "threatening" grid, so I was not particularly apprehensive.

After a good start into third place I found it impossible to hold off Senna, Schumacher and Jean as the car was not handling well on full tanks. I let them through, hoping that the car would improve as it lightened. Even after five laps the brakes were beginning to fade - maybe I pushed the car too hard when it was heavy with fuel.

As was often the case this year, I ended up in close company with a Ligier, in this case Brundle. It has been inevitable given the similarity of our cars' performance, but in Canada it was not much of a fight as Martin did not seem to be able to push me that hard.

At the time I was not very impressed with fourth place, but with hindsight any finish in the points this year must be considered a good result."

Gerhard Berger

FINISHING ORDER

	DRIVER	CAR	AVERAGE	DELAY
1	**Alain Prost**	Williams	189.667	—
2	**Michael Schumacher**	Benetton	189.193	14"527
3	**Damon Hill**	Williams	187.960	52"685
4	**Gerhard Berger**	Ferrari	186.742	1 lap
5	**Martin Brundle**	Ligier	186.627	1 lap
6	**Karl Wendlinger**	Sauber	185.062	1 lap
7	**J.J. Lehto**	Sauber	184.810	1 lap
8	**Erik Comas**	Larrousse	184.540	1 lap
9	**Christian Fittipaldi**	Minardi	184.161	2 laps
10	**Johnny Herbert**	Lotus	183.650	2 laps
11	**Alessandro Zanardi**	Lotus	182.296	2 laps
12	**Thierry Boutsen**	Jordan	182.287	2 laps
13	**Aguri Suzuki**	Footwork	180.261	3 laps
14	**Michael Andretti**	McLaren	179.543	3 laps
15	**Luca Badoer**	Lola Bms	178.110	4 laps
16	**Derek Warwick**	Footwork	178.101	4 laps
17	**Ukyo Katayama**	Tyrrell	174.140	5 laps
18	**Ayrton Senna**	McLaren	189.159	7 laps

RETIREMENTS

DRIVER	CAR	LAPS	REASON
Philippe Alliot	Larrousse	8	Gear
Rubens Barrichello	Jordan	10	Electronics
Mark Blundell	Ligier	13	Accident
Jean Alesi	Ferrari	23	Engine
Fabrizio Barbazza	Minardi	33	Gear
Andrea De Cesaris	Tyrrell	45	About-face
Riccardo Patrese	Benetton	52	Diseases

BEST LAPS

DRIVER	LAP	TIME	AVE.
Schumacher	57	1'21"500	195.681
Prost	61	1'21"613	195.410
Senna	57	1'22"015	194.452
Hill	54	1'22"101	194.249
Berger	57	1'22"776	192.665
Brundle	59	1'22"842	192.511
Andretti	49	1'22"957	192.244
Wendlinger	53	1'23"377	191.276
Lehto	41	1'23"447	191.115
Patrese	48	1'23"778	190.360
Herbert	54	1'24"359	189.049
Fittipaldi	43	1'24"674	188.346
Alesi	21	1'24"745	188.188
Comas	58	1'24"791	188.086
Boutsen	54	1'24"874	187.902
Zanardi	57	1'25"038	187.540
Suzuki	53	1'25"614	186.278
De Cesaris	44	1'25"763	185.954
Barbazza	23	1'25"832	185.805
Katayama	62	1'25"833	185.803
Blundell	13	1'26"236	184.934
Badoer	47	1'26"440	184.498
Barrichello	9	1'26"579	184.202
Warwick	54	1'26"579	184.036
Alliot	8	1'26"825	183.680

► *Prost and Schumacher celebrate another successful Sunday drive.*

▼ *Patrese and Brundle had a close battle during the early laps.*

FRANCE

Tha race of:

Martin Brundle

4 July 1993 • Circuit: Magny-Cours •
Length: 306,000 km • Organiser: Asa
Nevers Magny-Cours • Race Director:
Roland Bruynseraede • Spectators:
70.000 • Weather: sunny all three days

D. Hill Williams 1'14"382 (205,695)	**A. Prost** Williams 1'14"524 (205,303)
M. Brundle Ligier 1'16"169 (200,869)	**M. Blundell** Ligier 1'16"203 (200,779)
A. Senna McLaren 1'16"264 (200,619)	**J. Alesi** Ferrari 1'16"662 (199,577)
M. Schumacher Benetton 1'16"720 (199,426)	**R. Barrichello** Jordan 1'17"168 (198,269)
E. Comas Larrousse 1'17"170 (198,264)	**P. Alliot** Larrousse 1'17"190 (198,212)
K. Wendlinger Sauber 1'17"315 (197,892)	**R. Patrese** Benetton 1'17"362 (197,772)
A. Suzuki Footwork 1'17"441 (197,570)	**G. Berger** Ferrari 1'17"456 (197,532)
D. Warwick Footwork 1'17"598 (197,170)	**M. Andretti** McLaren 1'17"659 (197,015)
A. Zanardi Lotus 1'17"706 (196,896)	**J.J. Lehto** Sauber 1'17"812 (196,628)
J. Herbert Lotus 1'17"862 (196,502)	**T. Boutsen** Jordan 1'17"997 (196,161)
U. Katayama Tyrrell 1'19"143 (193,321)	**L. Badoer** Lola Bms 1'19"493 (192,470)
C. Fittipaldi Minardi 1'19"519 (192,407)	**F. Barbazza** Minardi 1'19"691 (191,992)
A. De Cesaris Tyrrell 1'19"856 (191,595)	

Prost's run of seven consecutive pole positions ended at Magny Cours. Hill, who had been quickest in three of the four practice sessions, was in pole position for the first time in his F1 career. The two Ligiers were on the second row. Perhaps not a surprise, given that the track is in the team's backyard and they have completed thousands of kilometers there. Nonetheless, an excellent show by both Brundle and Blundell. Senna, an unaccustomed fifth was joined on the third row by Alesi, who hauled the Ferrari to a grid position it did not deserve. After a clean start, the front of the field filed through the first corner in grid order, apart from Schumacher, who passed Alesi. During the early laps Hill, Prost and Brundle were each separated by a second and a half, while Blundell had his mirrors full of McLaren and Benetton. Despite constant pressure from Prost, Hill appeared comfortable at the head of field. When Hill came in for tyres, Prost put in his fastest lap to date, came in for his own stop and managed to get out just ahead of his teammate, where he stayed despite Hill's best efforts, going on to win his sixth French GP. Brundle lost his hard earned third position during the pitstops when he was passed by both Senna and Schumacher. Schumacher bided his time and with ten laps to go passed Senna to take third position.

Ligier, led by new owner Cyrille de Rouvre, has enjoyed its best season in over a decade. Part of the credit must go to Martin Brundle. At Magny Cours expectations of the team were high and Brundle did not disappoint, qualifying third after a tremendous effort. He held that position comfortably until lap 47 and the second round of pitstops. A lightening pitstop of 6.1 did not prevent him from being pushed back to fifth position by Senna and Schumacher, where he remained.

"I was very confident going to Magny Cours. We'd done a lot of kilometers around there and produced some good times, but, because it was the teams home GP, I was feeling the pressure. It is a very technical track. Setting up the car is very difficult and in many places you cannot see the track. At three places you come over blind brows and have to turn just over the top. You really need a lot of confidence in the circuit and in the car to get the best lap times. There's no doubt we had a great start going there. We'd just introduced some new aerodynamics to the car and that proved to a big help towards getting us to the front of the grid.

I start to prepare for the race on the Monday or Tuesday before. I look through data from last year's race, trying to apply it to my car and my situation. On Thursday we have a briefing with Goodyear and get to know what they're expecting. We're restricted to seven sets of tyres for the whole weekend. You need at least three sets available for the race, plus an emergency set, so you need to think it through very carefully before you start the weekend. At the start of the race it's total reflex action. You're accelerating to 100mph in two seconds. You're on full tanks of fuel. There are cars starting all around you. You're almost driving outside of yourself, as you have to react so much. As you're accelerating, cars are moving, maybe somebody has stalled in front of you, so you have no chance to think things through. You tend to take it as it comes. I made a good start. I think Mark tried to come around the outside of me into the Adelaide Hairpin, but I put a few manners on him there. We were running third and fourth and what surprised me was that I was running away from Senna and Schumacher and while Mark was doing a good rearguard action I pulled out a nice 10sec cushion.

The tyre wear rates suggest that you can get away with one stop, but we've found that the tyres have been going away very quickly. I was driving the race as a one race stop. The car was sliding around a lot, but I did not want to come in any earlier than I had to. I got held up by Berger. I was trying to lap him and he had just come out of the pits on fresh tyres. I was as quick as him, but no quicker and I could not pass him. That was the one point when the pressure got to us. We panicked a bit and came in three to four laps early. I was committed then to two tyre stops and that cost me third place in the race.

Senna then reeled me in a bit, but could not pass me. There is a point of no return if you stop for tyres ten laps before the end. Then you can't make up enough time in the final ten laps to compensate for the time in the pits. These things are constantly in your mind as you are hurtling around. So I stopped twice. Schumacher stopped for a second set and got out of the pits ahead of me and we both reeled Senna in and Schumacher managed to pass Senna. It was now near the end of the race and, becau-

se the fuel load had lightened, my car was running 2 to 3mm too high that's worth an awful lot of lap time. I was trying to lap Andretti, who was doing a very good job of barging me out of the way, protecting Senna's flank. I could not pass Senna and was right behind the pair of them. Senna's tyres had gone completely and in normal circumstances I would have got past him, but I had lapped Andretti once and he charged back past me on the way out of a hairpin. It was all very frustrating. It was totally against the regulations. In America you are allowed to do that - fighting not lose a lap -, but in F1 when they wave blue flags at you, you are obliged to pull over for the leaders who are lapping you.

I was absolutely devastated to finish fifth, after starting third and running a strong third, but at the end of the day to have the two Williams, Schumacher and Senna in front of me, I did not feel there was anybody in front of me that should not have been and I came away with two World Championship points and the satisfaction that we had done a good job."

Martin Brundle

FINISHING ORDER

	DRIVER	CAR	AVERAGE	DELAY
1.	**Alain Prost**	Williams	186.231	-
2.	**Damon Hill**	Williams	186.220	0.342
3.	**Michael Schumacher**	Benetton	185.565	21.209
4.	**Ayrton Senna**	McLaren	185.216	32.405
5.	**Martin Brundle**	Ligier	185.173	33.795
6.	**Michael Andretti**	McLaren	182.633	1 lap
7.	**Rubens Barrichello**	Jordan	182.526	1 lap
8.	**Christian Fittipaldi**	Minardi	181.518	1 lap
9.	**Philippe Alliot**	Larrousse	180.649	2 laps
10.	**Riccardo Patrese**	Benetton	180.630	2 laps
11.	**Thierry Boutsen**	Jordan	180.107	2 laps
12.	**Aguri Suzuki**	Footwork	180.091	2 laps
13.	**Derek Warwick**	Footwork	179.715	2 laps
14.	**Gerhard Berger**	Ferrari	179.670	2 laps
15.	**Andrea De Cesaris**	Tyrrell	175.309	4 laps
16.	**Erik Comas**	Larrousse	181.786	6 laps

BEST LAPS

DRIVER	LAP	TIME	AVE.
Schumacher	47	1'19"256	193.045
Brundle	49	1'19"919	191.444
Senna	58	1'20"521	190.013
Prost	41	1'20"530	189.991
Hill	35	1'20"542	189.963
Patrese	52	1'20"626	189.765
Andretti	61	1'20"631	189.753
Alliot	64	1'21"737	187.186
Berger	69	1'21"898	186.818
Comas	61	1'22"024	186.531
Barrichello	52	1'22"105	186.347
Suzuki	67	1'22"420	185.635
Fittipaldi	44	1'22"446	185.576
Boutsen	59	1'22"738	184.921
Warwick	58	1'22"867	184.633
Alesi	35	1'22"917	184.522
Blundell	6	1'22"939	184.473
De Cesaris	59	1'24"065	182.002
Wendlinger	3	1'24"376	181.331
Lehto	7	1'24"735	180.563
Herbert	4	1'25"136	179.712
Badoer	4	1'25"196	179.586
Barbazza	9	1'25"286	179.396
Katayama	4	1'25"933	178.046
Zanardi	2	1'26"538	176.801

RETIREMENTS

DRIVER	CAR	LAPS	REASON
Alessandro Zanardi	Lotus	3	Suspension
Ukyo Katayama	Tyrrell	9	Engine
Fabrizio Barbazza	Minardi	16	Gear
Johnny Herbert	Lotus	16	Went off track
Mark Blundell	Ligier	20	Went off track
J.J. Lehto	Sauber	22	Gear
Karl Wendlinger	Sauber	25	Gear
Luca Badoer	Lola Bms	28	Suspension
Jean Alesi	Ferrari	47	Engine

▲ *The battle for the minor placings can often be as intense as at the head of the field, here De Cesaris and Christian Fittipaldi do battle.*

▶ *The Footwork of Aguri Suzuki heads down to the final corner at Magny Cours after being lapped by Schumacher.*

▶▶ *The promise shown in qualifying did not materialise during the race for Martin Brundle, here he battles with his old F3 adversary Ayrton Senna.*

GREAT BRITAIN

The race of:

Riccardo Patrese

11 July 1993 • Circuit: Silverstone • Length: 308,334 Km • Organiser: Rac Motorsport Association • Race Director: Roland Bruynseraede • Spectators: 70.000 • Weather: Friday rain, Saturday variable, Sunday clear

A. Prost Williams 1'19"006 (238,129)	**D. Hill** Williams 1'19"134 (237,744)
M. Schumacher Benetton 1'20"401 (233,997)	**A. Senna** McLaren 1'21"986 (229,473)
R. Patrese Benetton 1'22"364 (228,420)	**M. Brundle** Ligier 1'22"421 (228,262)
J. Herbert Lotus 1'22"487 (228,080)	**D. Warwick** Footwork 1'22"834 (227,124)
M. Blundell Ligier 1'22"885 (226,984)	**A. Suzuki** Footwork 1'23"077 (226,460)
M. Andretti McLaren 1'23"114 (226,359)	**J. Alesi** Ferrari 1'23"203 (226,117)
G. Berger Ferrari 1'23"257 (225,970)	**A. Zanardi** Lotus 1'23"533 (225,224)
R. Barrichello Jordan 1'23"635 (224,949)	**J.J. Lehto** Sauber 1'24"071 (223,782)
E. Comas Larrousse 1'24"139 (223,601)	**K. Wendlinger** Sauber 1'24"525 (222,580)
C. Fittipaldi Minardi 1'24"664 (222,215)	**P. Martini** Minardi 1'24"718 (222,073)
A. De Cesaris Tyrrell 1'25"254 (220,677)	**U. Katayama** Tyrrell 1'25"343 (220,447)
T. Boutsen Jordan 1'25"363 (220,395)	**P. Alliot** Larrousse 1'25"397 (220,308)
L. Badoer Lola Bms 1'26"239 (218,157)	

Crowd numbers at Silverstone may not have been as great as they were in '92, but the spectators were unified in their support for Damon Hill. Mansell's heir did not disappoint when he provided spectators with a gripping battle for pole position with teammate Prost. Fastest on Saturday morning he lost out to Prost in the final minutes of the qualifying session and Prost took pole for the 28th time in his career. Despite having the latest series HB V8 Senna could not match Schumacher, who was third fastest in both Saturday sessions. Prost made a poor start and was passed by Senna, who took second, at the first corner. Hill pushed and at the end of the first lap had a lead of 1.4 seconds. This was extended as Prost was unable to pass his great rival's slower, but wider, car. He passed on lap 7 after several close calls, but Hill had a 7 second advantage. Schumacher overtook Senna on lap 10 to take third. Prost proceeded to make a succession of fastest laps and was on Hill's tail by lap 38 when the arrival of the safety car brought a truce. After the retrieval of Badoer's parked Lola, battle resumed. Hill successfully fought Prost off until heartbreak came on lap 42 when his engine blew. Prost cruised home after dealing with a minor challenge by Schumacher. Patrese inherited third after Senna ran out of fuel on the last lap.

Silverstone marked the true start of the season for Riccardo Patrese, who by now had become accustomed to a new car and a new team. He qualified fifth having gallantly given his car to Schumacher, who had spun into the gravel trap at Copse in his own car. What was an uneventful race for him before the safety car came out, when he was running 6th, became an eventful one after the safety car pulled off, when for six laps he was involved in a dogfight with Brundle and Herbert. He passed Herbert, Brundle retired and Patrese went on to inherit third from Senna.

"Silverstone is Benetton's home track. It is an advantage if you can test a lot of times at a circuit and because we did many kilometers there we went to the GP very well prepared. We knew that the car was performing very well there, especially in the fast corners. At that time our car was not in the best configuration for grip in slow corners, so coming to Silverstone where all of the corners are quite quick, we knew that we had a good chance of being very quick there.
After I had finished qualifying Michael was in need of a car because he'd spun in his car at Copse. We are a team, so I gave him mine. It was not a problem, of course you have to hurry up a little bit. By the end of practice, after the rain, we were in better shape.
As soon as I get into the car, it's easy for me to concentrate in a short period of time. On the grid it is better to be thinking of who is around you, because not all of the drivers react in the same way. You need to know what kind of reaction you will get from one driver to another driver so as to avoid accidents on the first corner.
I had a normal start. I was fifth at the start and sixth after the first lap, because Blundell went in front of me. So I said to myself "O.K. the race is very long. Wait until the pit stop because anything can happen after that." Then things got better and better, because the safety car came out and closed the gap between myself and Blundell. I still had to keep my concentration very high. You have to be very careful, sometimes the tyres can get cold and, of course, you are close to your competitors. It was the first time that I had driven with a safety car in such conditions. Now it should be the case that when the safety car is out the speed should be reduced, but there were two guys flat out for three laps to join the main group. So it was not really an easy situation. The normal lap time at Silverstone is 1.25. I was lapping at 1.30. It was not that I was going slow. What I am saying is that if you are not the first to join the pace car, and are just ahead of it, you have to drive very quickly and I just joined the group as the green flag came out. So really for me it was still a pure race even the lap I had behind the pace car. Then Blundell, myself and Herbert had a fight. Blundell had a problem with the gearbox and Senna ran out of fuel on the last lap, so my tactic to wait a little bit in the first part of the race meant it was a good result.
For me it was a race in two parts. The second part of that race was very exciting to do and maybe also to watch. Herbert passed me on lap 42 because somebody spun off in front of me at Bridge. I had to slow down so he caught me. I repassed him on the inside at Bridge again four laps later, when we were caught in traffic. It was pretty wild. We were in among lapped cars and Martin seemed to have a pretty wide car. I think it was a fair battle and very enjoyable for me.

I was surprised to see Senna at the side of the track. A race is never ever finished until the last lap. I did not expect to be on the podium when with one lap to go I was fourth. It was good to have my first podium finish at Silverstone. It was something that came at the right moment. The season started not very well and we were halfway through the season. With a podium finish the second half of the season started very well and it is still going very well. We hope to finish the season at this standard."

Riccardo Patrese

FINISHING ORDER

	DRIVER	CAR	AVERAGE	DELAY
1.	**Alain Prost**	Williams	216.030	—
2.	**Michael Schumacher**	Benetton	215.708	7.660
3.	**Riccardo Patrese**	Benetton	212.821	1'17.482
4.	**Johnny Herbert**	Lotus	212.783	1'18.407
5.	**Ayrton Senna**	McLaren	213.439	1 lap
6.	**Derek Warwick**	Footwork	210.385	1 lap
7.	**Mark Blundell**	Ligier	210.275	1 lap
8.	**J.J. Lehto**	Sauber	210.232	1 lap
9.	**Jean Alesi**	Ferrari	209.275	1 lap
10.	**Rubens Barrichello**	Jordan	209.249	1 lap
11.	**Philippe Alliot**	Larrousse	207.143	2 laps
12.	**Christian Fittipaldi**	Minardi	208.767	3 laps
13.	**Ukyo Katayama**	Tyrrell	197.953	4 laps
14.	**Martin Brundle**	Ligier	212.203	6 laps

BEST LAPS

DRIVER	LAP	TIME	AVE.
Hill	41	1'22"515	228.002
Prost	52	1'22"534	227.950
Schumacher	51	1'22"873	227.017
Blundell	51	1'24"655	222.238
Senna	46	1'24"886	221.634
Patrese	48	1'25"172	220.889
Brundle	35	1'25"208	220.796
Warwick	57	1'25"222	220.760
Herbert	32	1'25"455	220.158
Lehto	54	1'25"547	219.921
Alesi	57	1'25"733	219.444
Barrichello	56	1'25"848	219.150
Fittipaldi	55	1'26"428	217.679
Zanardi	32	1'26"695	217.009
Wendlinger	18	1'27"836	214.190
Boutsen	30	1'27"885	214.071
Alliot	34	1'28"106	213.534
De Cesaris	42	1'28"320	213.016
Martini	27	1'28"494	212.597
Badoer	29	1'29"474	210.269
Suzuki	8	1'29"968	209.114
Berger	8	1'30"293	208.362
Katayama	23	1'30"819	207.155

RETIREMENTS

DRIVER	CAR	LAPS	REASON
Erik Comas	Larrousse	1	Transmission
Michael Andretti	McLaren	1	Accident
Aguri Suzuki	Footwork	8	About-face
Gerhard Berger	Ferrari	10	Suspension
Karl Wendlinger	Sauber	24	Went off track
Pierluigi Martini	Minardi	31	Diseases
Luca Badoer	Lola Bms	32	Electric system
Thierry Boutsen	Jordan	41	Sheet
Damon Hill	Williams	41	Engine
Alessandro Zanardi	Lotus	41	Suspension
Andrea De Cesaris	Tyrrell	—	Not classified

▶ *Patrese was involved in a frantic battle with Johnny Herbert's Lotus towards the end of the race which was eventually decided in Patrese's favour.*

▶ *Hill leads Prost and Blundell under yellow flags mid way through the race.*

▶▶ *Alesi and Blundell fight it out early on, here they enter Stowe corner with Berger in close proximity.*

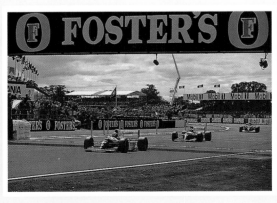

GERMANY
The race of:

Mark Blundell

25 July 1993 • Circuit: Hockenheim • Length: 306,675 km • Organiser: Ac Deutschland • Race Director: Roland Bruynseraede • Spectators: 148.000 • Weather: sunny all three days

A. Prost Williams 1'38"748 (248,451)	**D. Hill** Williams 1'38"905 (248,056)
M. Schumacher Benetton 1'39"580 (246,375)	**A. Senna** MCLaren 1'39"616 (246,286)
M. Blundell Ligier 1'40"135 (245,009)	**M. Brundle** Ligier 1'40"855 (243,260)
R. Patrese Benetton 1'41"101 (242,668)	**A. Suzuki** Footwork 1'41"138 (242,579)
G. Berger Ferrari 1'41"242 (242,330)	**J. Alesi** Ferrari 1'41"304 (242,182)
D. Warwick Footwork 1'41"449 (241,836)	**M. Andretti** MCLaren 1'41"531 (241,640)
J. Herbert Lotus 1'41"564 (241,562)	**K. Wendlinger** Sauber 1'41"642 (241,377)
A. Zanardi Lotus 1'41"858 (240,865)	**E. Comas** Larrousse 1'41"945 (240,659)
R. Barrichello Jordan 1'42"025 (240,470)	**J.J. Lehto** Sauber 1'42"032 (240,454)
A. De Cesaris Tyrrell 1'42"203 (240,052)	**C. Fittipaldi** Minardi 1'42"658 (238,988)
U. Katayama Tyrrell 1'42"682 (238,932)	**P. Martini** Minardi 1'42"786 (238,690)
P. Alliot Larrousse 1'42"910 (238,402)	**T. Boutsen** Jordan 1'42"007 (238,178)
L. Badoer Lola Bms 1'43"345 (237,399)	**M. Alboreto** Lola Bms 1'44"166 (235,528)

The Germans arrived at Hockenheim to support their national hero Schumacher and filled the stadium to capacity. On a circuit where power is essential on the long straights, a challenge to Williams-Renault was not expected. On Friday the crowds saw what they came for as Schumacher, fourth fastest in the morning, split the Williams pair. After Saturday's second qualifying session, however, the conventional order resumed with Prost taking pole and Hill second. The second row also had a familiar look about it. Having battled it out, Schumacher took third and Senna fourth. Rain has always caused problems at Hockenheim. The tree cover does not allow the mists to clear and the track to dry. The result is visibility problems and the worse case scenario of a car running into the back of another happened when in warm-up Warwick launched into the air after running into the back of Badoer. The wrecked Footwork ended upsidedown in a gravel trap, but Warwick, who had damaged his fingers, later declared his intention to race. Luckily, the circuit was dry for the race. Prost made a poor start, again, and was running third into the first corner. Schumacher took second to Hill. Prost's resolution to get back to the head of the field led to an exciting first lap. At the first chicane both he and Senna tried to outbrake each other. Prost fought off Senna, who spun to the back of the field. At the second chicane Prost used the escape road to avoid the spinning Brundle and fought his way past Schumacher and Hill. On lap 10 he was given a stop-go penalty, the controversial result of using the escape road, and he returned to sixth. By the time he had moved up to second both Williams had decided on only one tyre change. Their rivals took two. Hill was yet again denied victory when a rear tyre blew with only one lap to go. Prost gratefully inherited first, bringing him closer to winning the Driver's Championship. Schumacher received the loudest cheer of the day when he crossed the line in second.

Mark Blundell's fine third position once again confirmed the competitiveness of the Ligiers. Fourth after the first qualifying session, having had brake problems on Saturday morning, he dropped to fifth on the final grid. He ran with the frontrunners throughout and was briefly third when teammate Brundle and Prost were penalised. After pitting for tyres on lap 21 he came out best from a fight with Berger and went on to inherit 3rd when Hill retired.

"With Hockenheim being a very high speed track we felt quite confident that the car, with its Renault engine, was well suited to the circuit and that a good result was possible. We were very competitive from the beginning of practice on Friday, so we knew we had a good chance of running in the top six. We had some braking problems in practice which set us back a bit, but all in all the car was quite smooth running. You always get these niggly little problems during a GP weekend, but there were no major set backs.

Derek was very lucky not to have been badly hurt in the warm-up. It could have been a damn sight worse. I think that when conditions are as they were when Derek had his acci-

dent we should not run. Hockenheim is especially bad because of the amount of spray that comes off the cars. At those sort of speeds the water is thrown up and it just hangs like mist. It's very hard to see through it. Year in, year out the drivers complain and if the warm-up could have been put back an hour or so then that should have been done.

You're tuned into the GP all weekend from Friday. It's a case of sitting yourself down and planning a few tactics for the race. A lot is determined by where you have qualified, the handling of the car in race trim, consumption and tyre wear. You do have a mental file of some drivers' driving styles. There are some drivers that you can take care of quite easily, while others will be hard work and put up a fight. At the end of the day, if you've got to get by, you have got to try, regardless of who it is. At Hockenheim a large percentage of the lap is at full throttle. That's not particularly good for the engines, but reliability is a plus for us and on that basis we decided to run at a steady pace and wait for a few people to expire. Happily, that worked out.

After pitting for tyres on lap 21 I had a scrap with Gerhard. I overtook him fair and square the first time, but the active cars are much more superior under braking and he took me again. I overtook him the second time at 200mph with two wheels on the grass. You shouldn't have to do that. There is only a certain amount of driving that you can get away with without it looking quite blatant that you are not going to let someone by. I think that everybody saw at that point that Gerhard was not being very co-operative. What really annoyed me was the speeds we were achieving, 200/210mph, and if we had touched, and at one point we nearly did, the result could have been very bad indeed. We all accept a little bit of weaving. If you read the regulations you're only allowed to move the car once to make a block, after that you've got to let the guy go round you. I think Gerhard was having a strong defensive race, but when you're the guy trying to overtake at those speeds you don't see it that way.

I was running fourth when I saw the remainders of Damon's tyre. The board was showing me P3, so I just took it on board. I could not really relax because Senna was breathing down my neck. It was great to fight fairly and squarely with Senna and actually pull it off and finish in front of him. The last couple of laps I eased off just to make sure I came home. I was running strongly from the start, but finishing third was fantastic.

Martin and I get on well and at the end of it all it's for the good of the team. I'm sure it makes a difference when the two drivers communicate. We can share the information, we can get to a point a lot quicker and that reduces the time taken to develop the car. Not taking anything away from the team, we have both put in a tremendous amount of hard work."

Mark Blundell

FINISHING ORDER

	DRIVER	CAR	AVERAGE	DELAY
1	**Alain Prost**	Williams	233.861	—
2	**Michael Schumacher**	Benetton	233.038	16.664
3	**Mark Blundell**	Ligier	230.957	59.349
4	**Ayrton Senna**	McLaren	230.529	1'08.229
5	**Riccardo Patrese**	Benetton	229.414	1'31.516
6	**Gerhard Berger**	Ferrari	229.259	1'34.754
7	**Jean Alesi**	Ferrari	229.208	1'35.841
8	**Martin Brundle**	Ligier	228.639	1 lap
9	**Karl Wendlinger**	Sauber	228.372	1 lap
10	**Johnny Herbert**	Lotus	228.058	1 lap
11	**Christian Fittipaldi**	Minardi	227.521	1 lap
12	**Philippe Alliot**	Larrousse	226.257	1 lap
13	**Thierry Boutson**	Jordan	224.520	1 lap
14	**Pierluigi Martini**	Minardi	224.149	1 lap
15	**Damon Hill**	Williams	234.635	2 laps
16	**Michele Alboreto**	Lola Bms	221.057	2 laps
17	**Derek Warwick**	Footwork	218.050	3 laps

RETIREMENTS

DRIVER	CAR	LAPS	REASON
Erik Comas	Larrousse	1	Gear
Andrea De Cesaris	Tyrrell	1	Gear
Luca Badoer	Lola BMs	4	Suspension
Michael Andretti	McLaren	4	Suspension
Aguri Suzuki	Footwork	9	Gear
Alessandro Zanardi	Lotus	19	Went off track
J.J. Lehto	Sauber	22	Went off track
Ukyo Katayama	Tyrrell	28	About-face
Rubens Barrichello	Jordan	34	Wheel

BEST LAPS

DRIVER	LAP	TIME	AVE.
Schumacher	40	1'41"859	240.862
Senna	45	1'42"162	240.148
Prost	33	1'42"213	240.028
Brundle	36	1'42"331	239.751
Hill	39	1'42"574	239.183
Blundell	36	1'43"319	237.459
Alesi	40	1'44"222	235.401
Patrese	32	1'44"575	234.607
Barrichello	32	1'45"009	233.637
Wendlinger	38	1'45"128	233.373
Berger	33	1'45"489	232.574
Alliot	42	1'45"638	232.246
Herbert	41	1'45"767	231.963
Lehto	22	1'46"085	231.267
Zanardi	19	1'46"100	231.235
Katayama	26	1'46"186	231.047
Fittipaldi	29	1'46"323	230.750
Suzuki	8	1'47"183	228.898
Warwick	33	1'47"284	228.683
Martini	35	1'47"341	228.561
Boutsen	19	1'47"469	228.289
Andretti	3	1'47"505	228.213
Alboreto	40	1'48"875	225.341
Badoer	3	1'51"879	219.290
De Cesaris	1	2'38"437	154.850

▲ *The remnants of the disintegrated tyre which robbed Hill of victory at Hockenheim.*

▶ *Christian Fittipaldi confers with engineer Gustav Brunner at Minardi.*

▶▶ *Blundell and Schumacher, two drivers certain to visit the podium with regularity in the future.*

HUNGARY
The race of:
Damon Hill

15 August 1993 • Circuit: Hungaroring •
Length: 305,536 km • Organiser:
Magyar Autoklub • Race Director: Roland
Bruynseraede • Spectators: 30.000 •
Weather: nice weather all three days

A. Prost Williams 1'14"631 (191,406)	**D. Hill** Williams 1'14"835 (190,884)
M. Schumacher Benetton 1'15"228 (189,887)	**A. Senna** McLaren 1'16"451 (186,849)
R. Patrese Benetton 1'16"561 (186,581)	**G. Berger** Ferrari 1'16"939 (185,664)
P. Martini Minardi 1'17"366 (184,639)	**J. Alesi** Ferrari 1'17"480 (184,368)
D. Warwick Footwork 1'17"682 (183,888)	**A. Suzuki** Footwork 1'17"693 (183,862)
M. Andretti McLaren 1'18"107 (182,888)	**M. Blundell** Ligier 1'18"388 (182,232)
M. Brundle Ligier 1'18"392 (182,223)	**C. Fittipaldi** Minardi 1'18"446 (182,097)
J.J. Lehto Sauber 1'18"638 (181,653)	**R. Barrichello** Jordan 1'18"721 (181,461)
K. Wendlinger Sauber 1'18"840 (181,187)	**E. Comas** Larrousse 1'19"305 (180,125)
P. Alliot Larrousse 1'19"320 (180,091)	**J. Herbert** Lotus 1'19"444 (179,810)
A. Zanardi Lotus 1'19"485 (179,717)	**A. De Cesaris** Tyrrell 1'19"560 (179,548)
U. Katayama Tyrrell 1'20"270 (177,959)	**T. Boutsen** Jordan 1'20"482 (177,491)
M. Alboreto Lola Bms 1'21"502 (175,269)	**L. Badoer** Lola Bms 1'22"655 (172,824)

Practice at the Hungaroring on Friday saw Benetton mount a significant challenge to Williams-Renault. The dirty and dusty track, with its low grip surface, resulted in almost all but Hill spinning off during practice. At the end of the day Prost and Schumacher shared the front row, followed by their respective teammates on row two. Increased lappery on Saturday saw the times tumble and the old order returned, with Prost narrowly beating Hill for pole position. Schumacher claimed that his third position was a "strategic decision" to give him the better side of the grid. Sharing the second row was Senna, unhappy with his car's handling. When the green flag was waved for the final parade lap Prost's car stayed motionless. He had stalled and had to start from the back of the grid on one of the most difficult tracks on which to overtake.

Hill made a blinding start and was assisted by Schumacher, who held up the field when he ran wide at the first corner. No sooner had Schumacher passed Patrese and Berger, than he spun down the field to tenth and had to start another recovery drive. This time he got as far as Andretti's sixth place McLaren, when the American slowed suddenly with throttle problems and forced Schumacher to take avoiding action. He ended up in the gravel, from where he did not return.

Hill, meanwhile, was untroubled at the head of the field, almost a lap ahead of Patrese and Berger, his nearest pursuers once Senna had retired with the same problems as his teammate Andretti.

Hill's victory was the most popular of the year and richly deserved after his earlier disappointments.

Damon Hill achieved his first GP victory at Hungary on only his thirteenth GP start. He drove immaculately throughout the weekend. He led from the start and faced no opposition other than the searing heat and the battle to maintain a consistent pace and his own concentration. At Hungary he became the first second generation driver to win a GP.

"After all the recent disappointments I had been trying not to get over excited during the Hungarian GP about the prospect of actually winning. In Germany I was really confident that I was going to win, but I still had that niggling doubt. And naturally I felt very deflated that I'd done a lot of the work and not got the result. The Hungaroring is a track where you need as many laps as possible, and on Friday I lost time after doing five laps with the breaks locking on. They were so hot you could have made a cup of tea on them! The second qualifying session was very exciting because the times were very close and when you go round here you are just trying to find a few tenths. It's a very technical circuit rather like a big kart circuit. There are so many corners, and so many different types that it is almost better to find an average, rather than trying to be over good on one part than lose it on another. I actually enjoy driving on it, particularly during qualifying, but I have to admit I wasn't looking forward to the prospect of a race lasting an hour and fifty minutes in 35 degree with little chance of being able to overtake. I registered that Alain wasn't there any more and obviously my next concern was Schumacher. Fortunately I made probably the best start I've had since I've been in F1, which was vital, because the line into the first corner was extremely dirty, and it gave me the clearance I needed. Then I noticed that Schumacher had a problem at the corner, and I knew, yes, it was going to be tough, but not as tough as it might have been because he was behind Senna. Although I was not under any pressure from other drivers, the pressure was coming from whether or not I could actually do it, finish off the job for the first time. Because I was not being pushed and did not need to stretch the car to its limits this helped me on the fatigue side of things. At about the halfway stage I put in a quick lap, and I felt comfortable that I could have continued at those sort of lap times for a while. You're never going to come out of a race in that sort of heat feeling fresh, but I didn't feel bad. During the last laps, and at the same stage I had reached in Hockenhiem at the last race when the tyre blew, I just did not dare think about it. I try'd to concentrate totally on each corner, and on each gear change. But my mind was still wandering, and I was thinking to myself "what am I going to say at the end of this?" I kept telling myself that it's never over till it's over, and I thought of my dad, and what he might have said to me to keep my concentration up. And if you knew my dad, you know that just imagining him talking to me was enough to make me concentrate! When I actually took the chequered flag in the end I had difficulty believing it. I could hardly find

the words to explain how I felt at winning. In some ways it would have easier to have had to fight for the victory, but there are differnt degrees of difficulty, and having to drive in those conditions was as difficult as having to race anyone. The Hungaroring is a very difficult track and a lot of people made a lot of mistakes over the weekend. I managed to come through with a clean sheet. It meant a lot to me that Alain came over to congratulate me at the end after he had had such a dreadful race. It is important that you have a lot of regard for your teammate and he appreciates that I want to win, and I respect his record enormously. He's one of the greats in the sport, so to be in the same team as him is a privalege. It was only during the television interviews when I was sitting in the middle chair with Riccardo and Gerhard on either side and the questions were being asked about me winning my first GP, that it all began to sink in."

Damon Hill

FINISHING ORDER

	DRIVER	CAR	AVERAGE	DELAY
1.	**Damon Hill**	Williams	170.292	-
2.	**Riccardo Patrese**	Benetton	168.416	1'11"915
3.	**Gerhard Berger**	Ferrari	168.259	1'18"042
4.	**Derek Warwick**	Footwork	167.359	1 lap
5.	**Martin Brundle**	Ligier	167.240	1 lap
6.	**Karl Wendlinger**	Sauber	166.598	1 lap
7.	**Mark Blundell**	Ligier	166.579	1 lap
8.	**Philippe Alliot**	Larrousse	165.584	2 laps
9.	**Thierry Boutsen**	Jordan	164.495	2 laps
10.	**Ukyo Katayama**	Tyrrell	160.143	4 laps
11.	**Andrea De Cesaris**	Tyrrell	157.351	5 laps
12.	**Alain Prost**	Williams	153.831	7 laps

RETIREMENTS

DRIVER	CAR	LAPS	REASON
Rubens Barrichello	Jordan	1	Accident
Michael Andretti	McLaren	15	Accelerator
Ayrton Senna	McLaren	17	Accelerator
J.J. Lehto	Sauber	18	Engine
Jean Alesi	Ferrari	22	Accident
Christian Fittipaldi	Minardi	22	Accident
Michael Schumacher	Benetton	26	Injection
Luca Badoer	Lola Bms	37	About-face
Johnny Herbert	Lotus	38	About-face
Michele Alboreto	Lola Bms	39	Engine
Aguri Suzuki	Footwork	41	About-face
Alessandro Zanardi	Lotus	45	Gear
Erik Comas	Larrousse	54	Oil pressure
Pierluigi Martini	Minardi	59	Went off track

BEST LAPS

DRIVER	LAP	TIME	AVE.
Prost	52	1'19"633	179.383
Hill	54	1'20"441	177.581
Brundle	69	1'20"702	177.007
Berger	71	1'20"917	176.536
Patrese	32	1'21"101	176.136
Martini	59	1'21"939	174.335
Schumacher	20	1'22"031	174.139
Blundell	50	1'22"275	173.623
Comas	51	1'22"628	172.881
Wendlinger	59	1'22"745	172.636
Boutsen	53	1'22"754	172.618
Alliot	57	1'22"757	172.611
Senna	3	1'22"838	172.443
Warwick	42	1'23"202	171.688
De Cesaris	49	1'23"478	171.121
Suzuki	33	1'23"749	170.567
Katayama	50	1'23"764	170.536
Herbert	34	1'23"800	170.463
Zanardi	22	1'23"876	170.309
Alesi	3	1'24"020	170.017
Badoer	29	1'24"568	168.915
Andretti	9	1'24"667	168.717
Fittipaldi	14	1'24"850	168.354
Lehto	6	1'25"444	167.183
Alboreto	21	1'27"289	163.649

▶ *Damon Hill lines up to lap Herbert, the Lotus driver once again suffering from the bad luck which plagued him last year.*

▼ *The noticeable absence of Prost provided Hill with his best opportunity to date to clinch his first victory, he responded and kept cool under pressure.*

BELGIUM

The race of:

Michael Schumacher

29 August 1993 • Circuit: Spa Francorchamps • Length: 306,856 Km • Organiser: Royal Automobil Club de Belgique • Race Director: Roland Bruynseraede • Spectators: 70.000 • Weather: Friday and Saturday cloudy, Sunday sunny

▓▓▓▓▓▓▓▓▓▓▓▓▓▓

A. Prost Williams 1'47"571 (233,394)	**D. Hill** Williams 1'48"466 (231,468)
M. Schumacher Benetton 1'49"075 (230,176)	**J. Alesi** Ferrari 1'49"825 (228,604)
A. Senna McLaren 1'49"934 (228,377)	**A. Suzuki** Footwork 1'50"329 (227,559)
D. Warwick Footwork 1'50"628 (226,944)	**R. Patrese** Benetton 1'51"017 (226,149)
J.J. Lehto Sauber 1'51"048 (226,086)	**J. Herbert** Lotus 1'51"139 (225,901)
M. Brundle Ligier 1'51"350 (225,473)	**K. Wendlinger** Sauber 1'51"440 (225,291)
R. Barrichello Jordan 1'51"711 (224,744)	**M. Andretti** McLaren 1'51"833 (224,499)
M. Blundell Ligier 1'51"916 (224,333)	**G. Berger** Ferrari 1'52"080 (224,004)
A. De Cesaris Tyrrell 1'52"647 (222,877)	**P. Alliot** Larrousse 1'52"907 (222,364)
E. Comas Larrousse 1'53"186 (221,815)	**T. Boutsen** Jordan 1'52"465 (221,270)
P. Martini Minardi 1'53"526 (221,151)	**C. Fittipaldi** Minardi 1'53"942 (220,344)
U. Katayama Tyrrell 1'54"551 (219,172)	**L. Badoer** Lola Bms 1'54"978 (218,358)
M. Alboreto Lola Bms 1'55"965 (216,500)	

Williams-Renault dominated the practice at Spa. The high speed road circuit suited Prost's smooth and flowing driving style and he claimed his almost customary pole position after another close fought battle with Hill. Despite being unhappy with the handling of his Benetton, Schumacher headed the second row and was joined by Alesi. This was the first sign of an improvement in Ferarri's fortunes following months of testing and development. Another surprise was the form shown by both Footworks. Suzuki qualified sixth, his best performance to date, one place ahead of Warwick. The surprise of the warm-up was the speed of Schumacher's Benetton, only 4/10ths of a second behind the Williams duo. However, any hopes of a challenge for the lead were surely gone after a malfunction in the Benetton's new automatic start system. Prost took advantage of his starting position and held first at the first corner and began to pull away from the field. Alesi's promise did not last long and he retired on lap 4 with handling difficulties. Tyre stops started early, Hill being first to change. He was followed by Prost, who completed his stop without losing the lead. During the second set of stops Hill took the lead from Prost on lap 30. Afterwards Prost complained of deteriorating handling and traffic. He then came under pressure from Schumacher and on lap 32 slipped back into third. Hill resisted the challenge from Schumacher and went on to win an immensely satisfying second GP victory, Renault's 50th GP and the Constructors' Championship for Williams.

Michael Schumacher has displayed superb driving skills at each of the last three GPs at Spa. In 1991 he made his memorable GP debut with Jordan, in 1992 he won his first GP with Benetton and in 1993 he achieved second position. He qualified third, but technical problems left him stranded on the grid and he slipped back to eleventh position. He carved his way up through the field to third by lap 12. Lap 13 saw a controversial manoeuvre by Senna, which nearly forced Schumacher off. Schumacher passed Senna on the grass and on lap 32 passed Prost for second.

"I was hopeful of a good result. Spa is a driver's circuit. Our car is very good in high speed corners and there are a lot those, so I was thinking it could be a circuit for us. Unfortunately, the practice did not go as I expected. We had problems finding a good set-up. It took a while, but we got on top of it and in the end had a fantastic set-up for the race. The Williams were quick and we could not get anywhere close to them. When I could have done a quicker time than I did and qualified in second place, there were yellow flags on the lap and I had to brake. On Saturday when we drove on full tanks we were a lot quicker than Williams, which was surprising. The race showed again that we were really competitive against the Williams and that was something which impressed me and was good for the team and also good for the spectators.

On the grid the car just did not do what we expected it to do. When I released the clutch the revs just dropped right down and it was like starting a road car in fifth gear. It was not amusing and it was very tight between me and the drivers behind me when they were passing me, so I was very lucky that nobody hit me and that there was no accident. It was not just one problem, but a couple that came together. There was no time to work out what to do. It was a case of quickly making the best out of the situation. I was very close to stalling the engine, in fact I thought at first that it had stalled, so I was lucky because there was nothing I could do to make it better. I tried a few things, but I could not do much, just go through the procedure and wait until everything came back to normal.

It was still a good race for me - to come through from eleventh, passing a lot of people, which was not easy because a lot of cars in front of me had more power. The car was very good in the corners, then I could get into their slipstreams and beat them into the corners at the end of the straights. The first lap was especially good. I started eleventh and came back in eighth, so I passed three cars in the first lap, and that was quite nice and I have to say that there were a lot of good drivers in the field who fought, but fought fairly.

When Senna was exiting the pit he was looking for different lines. He turned left right across in front of me and I had to find a way through. I would have crashed into him if I had not gone across the grass. I was a bit upset because it was not necessary for him to do these things.

After the second tyre stop I came out of the pits behind Prost and I was much quicker through Eau Rouge, which gave me good speed up the hill. I got in the slipstream and outbraked Prost to pass him. At the time I was thinking that maybe I

could do the same with Damon, but he was much quicker through Eau Rouge. There was no other way to pass him, no way at all. I was not even close, because every time he had a clear track he could disappear a bit. I was absolutely over the limit, locking front wheels when I passed Prost, and there were big vibrations and that did not help me go quicker. I lost some performance because of this, but I fought until the end, although there was no way I could catch Damon.

I enjoyed this race very much. Coming from eleventh to second and beating one of the Williams, especially Prost, and having to fight all the way as nobody fell out of the race, we could not have done anything better. If you take the time I lost at the start and the time I was behind Damon Hill at the end I could have won the race, but I was still very pleased with second place."

Michael Schumacher

FINISHING ORDER

	DRIVER	CAR	AVERAGE	DELAY
1	**Damon Hill**	Williams	217.795	-
2	**Michael Schumacher**	Benetton	217.637	3.668
3	**Alain Prost**	Williams	217.153	14.988
4	**Ayrton Senna**	McLaren	213.594	1'39.763
5	**Johnny Herbert**	Lotus	212.641	1 lap
6	**Riccardo Patrese**	Benetton	210.939	1 lap
7	**Martin Brundle**	Ligier	210.239	1 lap
8	**Michael Andretti**	McLaren	210.142	1 lap
9	**J.J. Lehto**	Sauber	209.933	1 lap
10	**Gerhard Berger**	Ferrari	209.668	2 laps
11	**Mark Blundell**	Ligier	209.656	2 laps
12	**Philippe Alliot**	Larrousse	206.599	2 laps
13	**Luca Badoer**	Lola Bms	203.974	2 laps
14	**Michele Alboreto**	Lola Bms	200.187	3 laps
15	**Ukyo Katayama**	Tyrrell	197.251	4 laps

BEST LAPS

DRIVER	LAP	TIME	AVE.
Prost	41	1'51"095	225.990
Hill	40	1'51"212	225.753
Schumacher	38	1'51"242	225.692
Blundell	34	1'54"059	220.118
Senna	34	1'54"185	219.875
Andretti	33	1'54"614	219.052
Berger	38	1'55"240	217.862
Herbert	37	1'55"334	217.684
Lehto	33	1'55"475	217.418
Brundle	40	1'55"478	217.413
Patrese	34	1'55"681	217.031
Wendlinger	27	1'56"632	215.262
Comas	34	1'57"134	214.339
Alliot	34	1'57"390	213.872
Warwick	19	1'58"396	212.054
Suzuki	13	1'58"780	211.369
De Cesaris	24	1'58"866	211.216
Badoer	35	1'59"228	210.575
Alesi	3	1'59"283	210.478
Barrichello	7	1'59"554	210.001
Martini	10	2'00"006	209.210
Katayama	36	2'00"111	209.027
Fittipaldi	14	2'00"292	208.712
Alboreto	31	2'00"927	207.616

RETIREMENTS

DRIVER	CAR	LAPS	REASON
Thierry Boutsen	Jordan	1	Gear
Jean Alesi	Ferrari	4	Suspension
Rubens Barrichello	Jordan	11	Wheel
Aguru Suzuki	Footwork	14	Gear
Pierluigi Martini	Minardi	15	About-face
Christian Fittipaldi	Minardi	15	Wheel
Andrea De Cesaris	Tyrrell	24	Engine
Karl Wendlinger	Sauber	27	Engine
Derek Warwick	Footwork	28	Suspension
Erik Comas	Larrousse	37	Electric system

▶ *Thierry Boutsen and friends celebrate his ten years in Grand Prix racing, a week later he announced his retirement.*

▶ *Damon Hill catches Alain Prost for the lead at Spa, Fittipaldi's Minardi lies stricken at trackside.*

▶▶ *Alessandro Zanardi suffered a monumental accident at Eau Rouge he was fortunate to escape.*

ITALY
Tha race of:

Jean Alesi

12 September 1993 • Circuit: Monza •
Length: 307.4 Km • Organiser: Sias
Monza • Race Director: Giorgio Beghella
Bartoli • Spectators: 60.000 • Weather:
Friday and Saturday variable with rain;
Sunday sunny

A. Prost Williams 1'21"179 (257,209)	**D. Hill** Williams 1'21"491 (256,225)
J. Alesi Ferrari 1'21"986 (254,678)	**A. Senna** McLaren 1'22"633 (252,684)
M. Schumacher Benetton 1'22"910 (251,839)	**G. Berger** Ferrari 1'23"150 (251,112)
J. Herbert Lotus 1'23"769 (249,257)	**A. Suzuki** Footwork 1'23"856 (248,998)
M. Andretti McLaren 1'23"899 (248,871)	**R. Patrese** Benetton 1'23"918 (248,814)
D. Warwick Footwork 1'24"048 (248,429)	**M. Brundle** Ligier 1'24"137 (248,167)
J.J. Lehto Sauber 1'24"298 (247,693)	**M. Blundell** Ligier 1'24"344 (247,558)
K. Wendlinger Sauber 1'24"473 (247,180)	**P. Alliot** Larrousse 1'24"807 (246,206)
U. Katayama Tyrrell 1'24"886 (245,977)	**A. De Cesaris** Tyrrell 1'24"916 (245,890)
R. Barrichello Jordan 1'25"144 (245,232)	**E. Comas** Larrousse 1'25"257 (244,907)
M. Alboreto Lola Bms 1'25"368 (244,588)	**P. Martini** Minardi 1'25"478 (244,273)
M. Apicella Jordan 1'25"672 (243,720)	**C. Fittipaldi** Minardi 1'25"699 (243,643)
L. Badoer Lola Bms 1'25"957 (242,912)	**P. Lamy** Lotus 1'26"324 (241,879)

At Monza Ferrari made an unexpected challenge to Williams-Renault. To the delight of the tifosi, Alesi was third fastest after the final qualifying, with only 0.8 seconds separating him from Prost. For the twelfth time this season, pole position went to Prost.

Rain on Friday and Saturday morning restricted practice time for all the teams, but the race itself was dry. Two separate incidents under braking at the first corner caused confusion. Senna tangled with Hill, leaving Hill back in ninth, while in the midfield five drivers were forced into retirement in the squeeze approaching the first corner. For the first half of the race the race order was Prost, Schumacher, and Hill.

Schumacher's race ended on lap 22 in a cloud of smoke when his engine blew. Prost stopped for tyres on lap 26 and returned with his lead intact, a comfortable 20 seconds ahead of his teammate. Hill made inroads and by lap 45 both cars were together, but team orders applied for the last ten laps, as Prost well knew. On lap 49 Prost's hopes of clinching the World Championship at Monza died with his engine. Hill cruised over the line to take his third successive victory. Alesi drove a lonely race and inherited second position. Having spun on lap 2 and fallen back to 21st, Micheal Andretti took third position and his first podium finish after a stirring drive.

This high point in his F1 career was shortly followed by the announcement of his return to America. Fittipaldi's attempt to take Martini for seventh position ended in high drama, as he hit the back of his teammate's car and somersaulted into the air, crossing the line as his car landed back on its wheels.

Alesi was confident from the start and showed that confidence in qualifying when he was third fastest in both sessions on Friday and third again on the final qualifying on Saturday. As he celebrated cruising round the circuit after the chequered flag, teammate Berger came up from behind at speed. Both Ferraris moved to the left and to avoid a collision Berger swerved and hit the barriers at 203mph, tossing the car into the air and across to the otherside of the track. A superb start saw him split the Williams and run in second position before being passed by Schumacher and Hill. To the wild delight of the tifosi he inherited second position after the retirements of Schumacher and Prost.

"I talked to the Italian press in the week before Monza and I told them that we had a chance of beating everybody, even for the pole position and Williams in the race. We did a weeks testing at Monza before the race as it was very important for us to check everything. We had a new car to test, we had a 4-valve and a 5-valve engine, so we had a lot to confirm. We arrived at the Grand Prix having made a lot of progress with the chassis and the engine and with all the best solutions. Of course, Williams is the best, but we had the advantage of having done two or three long runs in testing and we knew exactly what would happen with fuel consumption and tyre wear. That was a good thing. After the weeks test, this is when I thought there was the possibility to

win. I said we could aim high and I think the result proved my point. I got the maximum out of the car and I was very satisfied.

After practice I was third, pushing very hard, so there was still the possibility of a win. I think, because it was raining on Friday and on Saturday morning, nobody really had the opportunity to work on their balance, so we kept our advantage. That is the reason why nobody was really catching me for third place. Of course, the Williams is still the Williams.

I am unhappy about what occured with Gerhard in practice and it took the edge off the pleasure I felt after my performance on Saturday. I was coming back slowly to the pits and when I saw Gerhard in my mirrors I decided to let him pass on the right and so I moved to the left. He hadn't seen the chequered flag and had started another qualifying run. I must admit it gave me a fright and I only relaxed when I got to the medical centre and saw him smiling and gave him a hug.

Before the start of the race I like to be alone to concentrate. I don't really worry about the other drivers around me on the grid. Some drivers make the start difficult. My car was very heavy at the beginning of the race, but I made a good start. The trouble is we have to carry 40 kilos of petrol compared to the others. For that reason I can't push the car too hard, in order not to damage the tyres and the brakes. That is why Schumacher and Hill were able to pass me. I knew that I would probably have to wait in the first part of the race and that only later would I be able to push harder.

I was prepared to let them go and chase them after the tyre laps.

I didn't see that it was Alain who had blown up. I just saw the flags waving. I waited until I went past the pits to hear what had happened and I was happy just to make one more place.

Qualifying third was great and it was thanks to the hard work of all the team. I was very satisfied to get second position. I was close to the Williams, but from the beginning I knew they were stronger. It was a very important race for Ferrari, as there is a special relationship between Italy and Ferrari, and I knew that I would have to do my very best. The support I get from the tifosi is wonderful and it gives me that added boost. The reception I got from them after practice for instance was fantastic, very special."

Jean Alesi

FINISHING ORDER

	DRIVER	CAR	AVERAGE	DELAY
1.	**Damon Hill**	Williams	239.144	-
2.	**Jean Alesi**	Ferrari	237.094	40.012
3.	**Michael Andretti**	McLaren	232.542	1 lap
4.	**Karl Wendlinger**	Sauber	231.660	1 lap
5.	**Erik Comas**	Larrousse	229.869	2 laps
6.	**Pierluigi Martini**	Minardi	229.491	2 laps
7.	**Christian Fittipaldi**	Minardi	229.433	2 laps
8.	**Philippe Alliot**	Larrousse	226.810	2 laps
9.	**Luca Badoer**	Lola Bms	226.596	2 laps
10.	**Pedro Lamy**	Lotus	229.061	4 laps
11.	**Alain Prost**	Williams	240.351	5 laps
12.	**Andrea De Cesaris**	Tyrrell	220.760	6 laps
13.	**Ukyo Katayama**	Tyrrell	209.622	6 laps

RETIREMENTS

DRIVER	CAR	LAPS	REASON
Rubens Barrichello	Jordan	0	Accident
Aguri Suzuki	Footwork	0	Accident
Derek Warwick	Footwork	0	Accident
J.J. Lehto	Sauber	0	Accident
Marco Apicella	Jordan	1	Accident
Ayrton Senna	McLaren	8	Accident
Martin Brundle	Ligier	8	Accident
Johnny Herbert	Lotus	14	Went off track
Gerhard Berger	Ferrari	15	Suspension
Mark Blundell	Ligier	20	Went off track
Michael Schumacher	Benetton	21	Engine
Michele Alboreto	Lola Bms	23	Suspension

BEST LAPS

DRIVER	LAP	TIME	AVE.
Hill	45	1'23"575	249.835
Prost	39	1'24"407	247.373
Alesi	47	1'24"140	245.243
Schumacher	21	1'25"969	242.878
Andretti	46	1'26"380	241.723
Patrese	31	1'27"309	239.151
Wendlinger	39	1'27"458	238.743
Alliot	43	1'27"534	238.536
Senna	5	1'27"939	237.437
Fittipaldi	46	1'28"062	237.106
Berger	9	1'28"139	236.899
Comas	39	1'28"192	236.756
Herbert	8	1'28"512	235.900
Brundle	7	1'28"559	235.775
De Cesaris	34	1'28"620	235.613
Blundell	12	1'28"889	234.900
Martini	43	1'28"907	234.852
Lamy	32	1'29"209	234.057
Badoer	34	1'29"426	233.489
Katayama	46	1'29"502	233.291
Alboreto	18	1'30"168	231.568

▶ *Damon Hill leads Senna during the early laps after Senna had made contact with the Englishman at the first chicane.*

▼ *Marco Apicella prepares for his debut with the Jordan Grand Prix team at Monza, his race unfortunately lasted a few thousand metres where he spun and retired at the Goodyear chicane.*

▶▶ *Pedro Lamy yet another Grand Prix debutante sits patiently in the Castrol Lotus before venturing out on the track for his qualifying run on the Saturday afternoon.*

PORTUGAL

Tha race of:

Alain Prost

26 September 1993 ● Circuit: Estoril ●
Length: km 308,850 km ● Organiser:
Automobil Club de Portugal ● Race Director:
Roland Bruynseraede ● Spectators: 55.000 ●
Weather: Friday sunny, Saturday sunny with
wind, Sunday good weather

D. Hill Williams 1'11"494 (219,039)		**A. Prost** Williams 1'11"683 (218,462)	
M. Hakkinen McLaren 1'12"443 (216,170)		**A. Senna** McLaren 1'12"491 (216,027)	
J. Alesi Ferrari 1'13"101 (214,224)		**M. Schumacher** Benetton 1'13"403 (213,343)	
R. Patrese Benetton 1'13"863 (212,014)		**G. Berger** Ferrari 1'13"933 (211,813)	
D. Warwick Footwork 1'14"388 (210,518)		**M. Blundell** Ligier 1'14"577 (209,984)	
M. Brundle Ligier 1'14"708 (209,616)		**J.J. Lehto** Sauber 1'14"833 (209,266)	
K. Wendlinger Sauber 1'15"016 (208,755)		**J. Herbert** Lotus 1'15"183 (208,292)	
R. Barrichello Jordan 1'15"433 (207,601)		**A. Suzuki** Footwork 1'15"491 (207,442)	
A. De Cesaris Tyrrell 1'15"904 (206,313)		**P. Lamy** Lotus 1'15"920 (206,270)	
P. Martini Minardi 1'15"942 (206,210)		**P. Alliot** Larrousse 1'16"144 (205,663)	
U. Katayama Tyrrell 1'16"186 (205,550)		**E. Comas** Larrousse 1'16"417 (204,928)	
E. Naspetti Jordan 1'16"566 (204,529)		**C. Fittipaldi** Minardi 1'16"651 (204,303)	
M. Alboreto Lola Bms 1'17"118 (203,065)		**L. Badoer** Lola Bms 1'17"739 (201,443)	

Alain Prost arrived in Portugal determined to secure his fourth World Championship after the disappointment of Monza. It was Damon Hill, however, who took pole position, with Prost second. Prost had spun off and hit the wall on his first lap of Saturday afternoon and had to wait to take over Hill's car at the end of the session before he could improve his time. On the second row Hakkinen, only 0.8 behind the Williams after a startling performance in qualfiying, was third, with Senna fourth. Hill's hard earned pole was lost when he failed to get away on the warm-up lap and he had to start at the back of the field. The charge at the first corner was not for the feinthearted. To everyone's disbelief Alesi led into the first corner from the third row and held off the McLarens until lap 20, when he came in for tyres. Prost led before his own stop from Schumacher, as Senna retired with engine failure on lap 20. Schumacher's decision to stop for tyres early paid dividends as he took the lead from Prost when Prost made his stop on lap 29. Schumacher, secure in the knowledge that Prost would not risk the World Championship with a rash overtaking manoeuvre, went on without a second change to win his third GP with Prost chasing just one second behind. Hill had carved his way through the field to take third, with Alesi fourth. Hakkinen, having made a stunning debut drive with McLaren, crashed on lap 33.

When Prost returned to F1 after his sabbatical year it was for one reason, a fourth World Championship and a first with Renault. Estoril saw him achieve that goal, but it also saw him announce his retirement and the end of a glittering career in which he scored more points than any other driver in history.

"I was under a lot of pressure at Estoril and the race was hard. I was exhausted after the race, but not just because of the race itself. It started badly when I had a crash on Saturday afternoon. On the morning of the race I did not like the car and the engine. I wanted to take the T car, so I took it for the first warm-up lap and then I changed back to the race car. I heard some strange noise on the engine. When I started on the formation lap I did not know whether Damon would be taking up his position or not. When I saw that he was not coming, I just concentrated on my start, because then the first lap would be easier for Hakkinen and Senna. Also, because Damon was not there, I just had the Championship to think about. I only asked the team where Damon was when there were about 10 or 15 laps to go.

I had a good start, with maybe too much wheelspin. Hakkinen pushed me onto the right and I had to brake before the corner, because I was almost on the grass. I tried to overtake Hakkinen once or twice, but he was weaving on the straight. There was no point in taking any risks. Under these conditions it can be difficult to know what to do. I was quicker, for sure, but it was sometimes taking two or three laps to find a way past much slower cars, like Martini's for example. Even with a lap speed differential of three or four seconds, it was very difficult. I think we saw the

limit of the modern F1 car. It was very difficult to overtake. If we are talking about rules again, there are so many things that should be changed, especially on the aerodynamic side, to allow more overtaking and to make the racing more open. But that is something else...

I wasn't surprised to see Alesi lead. When you are starting you can't see everybody. If Hakkinen had not been pushing me before the first corner, I would have been on the right line. I was beside Alesi, so I could have managed to be first into the first corner. He did a good start and did a very good first part of the race. I don't think he was as quick as the McLarens or my car, especially with a car full of fuel, but it was difficult to stay close behind him and Senna and Hakkinen did not manage to overtake him.

I think what Michael [Schumacher] did was very good. He stopped for tyres first. When Hakkinen and Alesi stopped for tyres he was behind me and I knew that I would have to push. Just after my pitstop I thought I would have to catch up a little bit and then Michael would stop again. I never imagined that he would only stop once, but, when it got to twenty laps from the end, I knew he was not going to and was going to try and do it on one set. I could see that he was going to be difficult to overtake. He was also weaving a little bit. To stay close behind another car on this track is very difficult. In the fast corners you get more and more understeer and in the low speed corners you cannot do what you want. Also my tyres were getting a bit old. I knew that I could be World Champion by staying behind Michael, but I wanted to win this one for my team, which has done a very good job this year. We had a fantastic ambience.

When I saw what Hakkinen did, I was thinking that if I did one-tenth of that I would have had a penalty. So I felt the fact I am retiring is very good as the rules are not the same for everyone. There is no temptation for me to go on at all, not even the temptation to try to equal Fangio. At the start of the year it was my challenge to win the fourth title and I have done it. If by luck I were to become World Champion next year, I would be asked why I didn't go for a sixth in 1995. There is no limit and I think it is good to stop."

Alain Prost

FINISHING ORDER

	DRIVER	CAR	AVERAGE	DELAY
1.	**Michael Schumacher**	Benetton	199.748	-
2.	**Alain Prost**	Williams	199.713	0"982
3.	**Damon Hill**	Williams	199.454	8"206
4.	**Jean Alesi**	Ferrari	197,351	1'07"605
5.	**Karl Wendlinger**	Sauber	195.350	1 lap
6.	**Martin Brundle**	Ligier	195.339	1 lap
7.	**J.J. Lehto**	Sauber	194.027	2 laps
8.	**Pierluigi Martini**	Minardi	193.706	2 laps
9.	**Christian Fittipaldi**	Minardi	193.148	2 laps
10.	**Philippe Alliot**	Larrousse	191.966	2 laps
11.	**Erik Comas**	Larrousse	191.038	3 laps
12.	**Andrea De Cesaris**	Tyrrell	190.788	3 laps
13.	**Rubens Barrichello**	Jordan	190.396	3 laps
14.	**Luca Badoer**	Lola Bms	188.401	3 laps
15.	**Derek Warwick**	Footwork	194.976	8 laps
16.	**Riccardo Patrese**	Benetton	194.958	8 laps

RETIREMENTS

DRIVER	CAR	LAPS	REASON
Emanuele Naspetti	Jordan	8	Engine
Ukyo Katayama	Tyrrell	12	Went off track
Ayrton Senna	McLaren	19	Engine
Aguri Suzuki	Footwork	27	Gear
Mika Hakkinen	McLaren	32	Accident
Gerhard Berger	Ferrari	35	Accident
Michele Alboreto	Lola Bms	38	Differential
Mark Blundell	Ligier	51	Accident
Johnny Herbert	Lotus	60	About-face
Pedro Lamy	Lotus	61	About-face

BEST LAPS

DRIVER	LAP	TIME	AVE.
Hill	68	1'14"859	209.193
Prost	45	1'15"780	206.651
Schumacher	56	1'16"201	205.509
Blundell	47	1'16"793	203.925
Alesi	51	1'16"806	203.890
Barrichello	39	1'17"114	203.076
Patrese	32	1'17"340	202.483
Brundle	40	1'17"638	201.705
Wendlinger	40	1'17"694	201.560
Lamy	59	1'17"758	201.394
Hakkinen	31	1'17"992	200.790
Lehto	47	1'18"069	200.592
Warwick	60	1'18"134	200.425
De Cesaris	53	1'18"290	200.026
Senna	17	1'18"365	199.834
Fittipaldi	68	1'18"581	199.285
Alliot	42	1'18"769	198.809
Martini	53	1'18"806	198.716
Herbert	31	1'18"961	198.326
Comas	43	1'19"014	198.193
Berger	31	1'19"568	196.813
Badoer	49	1'19"602	196.729
Suzuki	22	1'20"446	194.665
Alboreto	38	1'21"270	192.691
Katayama	5	1'21"563	191.999
Naspetti	4	1'22"756	189.231

▶ *Damon Hill pipped Alain Prost to pole position for the second time in his career, an impressive achievement which unfortunately he was not to capitalise on since Damon stalled his engine during the warm up lap. His pursuit of the leaders was one of the highlights of the 1993 season, he has developed with every passing Grand Prix and now certainly rates as one of the top ten.*

▶▶ *The Scicilian speed merchant Jean Alesi blasted past everyone at the green lights to lead the Portuguese Grand Prix, his performance was reminiscent of the late great Gilles Villeneuve, his hero and role model.*

▶ *Alain Prost chased here by Michael Schumacher emerged second in the fight to the flag which was enough for the championship, now the title has been settled he said, "We can go racing".*

JAPAN
Tha race of:

Eddie Irvine

24 October 1993 • Circiuit: Suzuka • Length: 310,792 km • Organiser: Suzuka Motors Club • Race Director: Roland Bruynseraede • Weather: Friday and Saturday sunny, Sunday variable with rain

A. Prost Williams 1'37"154 (217,288)	**A. Senna** McLaren 1'37"284 (216,998)
M. Hakkinen McLaren 1'37"326 (216,904)	**M. Schumacher** Benetton 1'37"530 (216,450)
G. Berger Ferrari 1'37"622 (216,246)	**D. Hill** Williams 1'38"352 (214,641)
T. Warwick Footwork 1'38"780 (213,711)	**E. Irvine** Jordan 1'38"966 (213,310)
A. Suzuki Footwork 1'39"278 (212,639)	**R. Patrese** Benetton 1'39"291 (212,611)
J.J. Lehto Sauber 1'39"391 (212,398)	**R. Barrichello** Jordan 1'39"426 (212,323)
U. Katayama Tyrrell 1'39"511 (212,141)	**J. Alesi** Ferrari 1'39"535 (212,090)
M. Brundle Ligier 1'39"951 (211,207)	**K. Wendlinger** Sauber 1'40"153 (210,782)
M. Blundell Ligier 1'40"696 (209,645)	**A. De Cesaris** Tyrrell 1'40"696 (209,645)
J. Herbert Lotus 1'41"488 (208,009)	**P. Lamy** Lotus 1'41"600 (207,780)
E. Comas Larrousse 1'41"769 (207,434)	**P. Martini** Minardi 1'41"989 (206,987)
T. Suzuki Larrousse 1'42"175 (206,610)	**J.M. Gounon** Minardi 1'43"812 (203,352)

In 1989 and 1990 the Japanese GP at Suzuka was the scene of the controversial showdowns for the title between Prost and Senna. Both incidents left ugly scars on the history of the race. After final practice in 1993 the front row was identical to that of '89 and '90. Prost held pole position from his great rival Senna after a captivating second session, in which less than half a second separated the top five. Hakkinen and Schumacher shared second row. The capacity crowd saw Senna lead to the first corner, with Prost content to follow in the early laps opening a gap to third place Hakkinen. On lap 13 Senna was among the first to call of tyres, but then the rain came. Initially, the leading runners stayed out in the hope that it was only a shower. They were disappointed. After the stops for wets, Senna, revelling in the conditions, comfortably led Prost and Hakkinen. Prost was aided in his chase of Senna by the battle for fifth between Hill and Irvine. The Brazilian was lapping both and when sandwiched between them was, to his annoyance, passed by Irvine, keen to continue his battle with Hill. The battle between Senna and the Irishman would continue after the chequered flap! By lap 41 the top three had changed to slicks, but this had no bearing on the final order. Senna gave McLaren its 103rd GP victory, equalling the all time record of Ferrari, and Hakkinen achieved his first F1 podium finish.

From the start Irvine's GP debut was sensational. Using his circuit knowledge to good effect, he was fifth after the first untimed practice. After the first official qualifying session he was eleventh, his best run having been disrupted by Alesi's accident. Saturday saw an improvement and a delighted eighth. A magnificent start saw him run fifth before being demoted by Schumacher and Hill. He ran as high as fourth during the pit stops, but ultimately lost places due to the timing of his own stops. His debut was not without controversy and there were incidents with both Senna and Warwick. By finishing sixth Irvine became the first driver to score points on his debut since Alesi in 1989.

"At the beginning I really wasn't optimistic. Before we got to Suzuka it was just awful. The car was so small, and although power wasn't a problem, the handling was not so good and it took a very certain technique to drive the car. Luckily we were able to make changes for Suzuka and it went well there.

My experience at Suzuka helped the whole team as I knew exactly how a good car should be round Suzuka and I was able to say what we need to do. As a result we got the car going very quickly. I think my experience helped Rubens as well. I wasn't surprised when I fifth in practice, because I wasn't anywhere near the limit of the car. I was also a bit pessimistic and thought, "It can't be this easy". After the first qualifying, when I was 11th, I thought that we should have had Katayama, that we should have been quicker than him and should have had tenth, but the downside could have been a lot worse. Rubens was half or seven tenths of a second slower than me and he was 19th.

After the first qualifying run, I didn't have the tyre pressures high enough. I did a very bad lap; I was slow and all over the place. There was no problem with the next set of tyres, but I didn't give it 100%. I had fallen back so far with the previous run, I knew I needed to be a bit conservative. That was disappointing, because I couldn't go into my last set of tyres and give it everything.

I hadn't made a racing start in F1 before, so on Saturday I tried three different types of start. We checked the computer to see which one was better. The middle one was, so I just did that one.

Looking around the grid, I'd never raced against Warwick and I didn't know what he was like, so I watched him. I knew Damon and Schumacher were good starters, so I was picking my place.

I knew I had to go round on the outside on the first corner. I made a good start, better than Schumacher, Damon and those guys, but I had to actually come off the power to get over to the other side of the circuit. That lost me a little bit of momentum and I should've been up into fourth after the second corner, instead of fifth.

I was forced back by Schumacher, Damon and Suzuki and after nine laps my back was in agony and I couldn't go full throttle. I lost time due to confusion in the pits. They wanted me to come in too early and I didn't want to come in. Then whenever I wanted to come in, Rubens had come in. Basically, I lost 40 seconds.

I diced with Damon and it was great. I was all over him, but I couldn't get past, because I was too slow out of the corners. Senna was behind me

for about five laps, he wasn't catching me and then someone spilt oil at Degner and I slipped wide. I stayed wide for Senna to go through and get on with it. He couldn't pull away from me. Then Damon came flying out of the pits, but Senna didn't seem to want to overtake Damon, or he kind of looked and Damon wouldn't let him go through. I think Senna was happy to stay; he was leading the race and had no need to take any risks. Obviously, I wasn't happy. I was fighting Damon for fourth place. So I had to go at him. I had no option. At one of the corners Senna braked down the inside and I drove around the outside. I didn't put him at risk. I went where Damon did and we had a good little battle until I got too close to him at one of the corners and just understeered wide again.

I wasn't really happy with sixth position, it should have been a lot better. To be honest, it wasn't a great performance. I didn't drive particularly well in the race. I was in such pain with my back. The car was just too small and I was bent over so much. What happened with Senna after the race really angered me. I had done a good job and all of a sudden the focus was on a fight.

As for F1 in the future, if it happens, it happens. I believe in destiny and always knew I would get to F1, if only for one race."

Eddie Irvine

FINISHING ORDER

	DRIVER	CAR	AVERAGE	DELAY
1.	**Ayrton Senna**	McLaren	185.612	-
2.	**Alain Prost**	Williams	185.260	11.435
3.	**Mika Hakkinen**	McLaren	184.811	26.129
4.	**Damon Hill**	Williams	183.075	1'23.538
5.	**Rubens Barrichello**	Jordan	182.729	1'35.101
6.	**Eddie Irvine**	Jordan	182.392	1'46.421
7.	**Mark Blundell**	Ligier	180.535	1 lap
8.	**J.J. Lehto**	Sauber	180.485	1 lap
9.	**Martin Brundle**	Liegier	180.389	2 laps
10.	**Pierluigi Martini**	Minardi	178.549	2 laps
11.	**Johnny Herbert**	Lotus	178.389	2 laps
12.	**Toshio Suzuki**	Larrousse	176.664	2 laps
13.	**Pedro Lamy**	Lotus	177.570	4 laps
14.	**Derek Warwick**	Footwork	181.098	5 laps

RETIREMENTS

DRIVER	CAR	LAPS	REASON
Andrea De Cesaris	Tyrrel	1	Accident
Jean Alesi	Ferrari	7	Electronics
Michael Schumacher	Benetton	10	Accident
Erik Comas	Larrousse	17	Engine
Karl Wendlinger	Sauber	25	Accelerator
Jena-Marc Gounon	Minardi	26	Whitdrawn
Ukyo Katayama	Tyrrell	26	Engine
Aguri Suzuki	Footwork	40	Went off track
Gerhard Berger	Ferrari	40	Engine
Riccardo Patrese	Benetton	45	Went off track

BEST LAPS

DRIVER	LAP	TIME	AVE.
Prost	53	1'41"176	208.650
Brundle	49	1'42"119	206.724
Hakkinen	13	1'43"158	204.641
Senna	15	1'43"217	204.524
Blundell	50	1'43"610	203.749
Herbert	51	1'44"144	202.704
Irvine	46	1'44"293	202.414
Hill	51	1'44"507	202.000
Warwick	46	1'44"761	201.510
Lehto	50	1'44"802	201.431
Lamy	49	1'45"389	200.309
Barrichello	49	1'45"578	199.951
Berger	15	1'45"648	199.818
Schumacher	3	1'45"988	199.177
Wendlinger	14	1'46"408	198.391
A. Suzuki	17	1'46"819	197.628
T. Suzuki	49	1'46"819	197.628
Patrese	5	1'47"373	196.608
Martini	50	1'47"533	196.316
Katayama	15	1'47"816	195.800
Alesi	5	1'47"823	195.788
Gounon	11	1'48"940	193.788
Comas	4	1'50"230	191.512

▶ *In Suzuka Senna and Irvine were the headline makers.*

▼ *The start was always going to be critical, especially with previous Prost/ Senna openings at Suzuka.*

AUSTRALIA

Interview at:

Charly Witing

7 November 1993 • Circuit: Adelaide •
Length: 298,620 km • Organiser:
Australian Formula One Gp Office • Race
Director: Roland Bruynseraede • Spectators:
78.000 • Weather: Friday and Saturday
sunny, Sunday cloudy.

A. Senna McLaren 1'13"371 (185,468)	**A. Prost** Williams 1'13"807 (184,373)
D.Hill Williams 1'13"826 (184,325)	**M. Schumacher** Benetton 1'14"098 (183,649)
M. Hakkinnen McLaren 1'14"106 (183,629)	**G. Berger** Ferrari 1'14"194 (183,411)
J. Alesi Ferrari 1'15"332 (180,640)	**M. Brundle** Ligier 1'16"022 (179,001)
R. Patrese Benetton 1'16"077 (178,871)	**A. Suzuki** Footwork 1'16"079 (178,867)
K. Wendlinger Sauber 1'16"106 (178,803)	**J.J. Lehto** Sauber 1'16"286 (178,381)
R. Barrichello Jordan 1'16"459 (177,978)	**M. Blundell** Ligier 1'16"469 (177,954)
A. De Cesaris Tyrrell 1'16"892 (176,975)	**P. Martini** Minardi 1'16"905 (176,946)
D. Warwick Footwork 1'16"919 (176,913)	**O. Katayama** Tyrrell 1'17"018 (176,686)
E. Irvine Jordan 1'17"341 (175,948)	**J. Herbert** Lotus 1'17"450 (175,700)
E. Comas Larrousse 1'17"750 (175,023)	**J. M. Gounon** Minardi 1'17"754 (175,014)
P. Lamy Lotus 1'19"369 (171,452)	**T. Suzuki** Larrousse 1'21"793

Australia marks the end of a long season and is one of the most popular races on the calendar. This season Adelaide saw the end of an era as the two greatest drivers of their generation raced together for the last time. The moods of both drivers contrasted starkly - Prost was reflective and Senna, who in the past had refused any efforts at a reconciliation with Prost, was alight. Here was an opportunity to defeat his great rival in possibly his last ever F1 race.

Senna's determination was evident in the first qualifying session when he finished half a second ahead of his great rival. The following day saw the track temperatures rise to the low 80's. In the hot conditions the only front-runner to improve his grid position was the impressive Hill, who moved up onto the second row. Senna won pole position, as he has done at Adelaide each year since the inception of the race. However, the Senna-Irvine incident at Japan cast a shadow over any celebration of such a remarkable record as questions continued to be asked by the press. The result - a five minute attack by the Brazilian on the ignorance of reporters and Irvine.

After two false starts, Prost was quick off the mark, but Senna used his pole position to great effect and led the field at the first corner, followed by Prost, Hill and Schumacher. Senna opened a comfortable gap, knowing full well that traffic and tyre stops would be crucial on the tortuos street circuit. His was a flawless performance. Prost's battle was with Hill, who made a powerfull challenge. An attack by Hill at the end of the Brabham Straight on lap 68 ended in near disaster. Prost braked very late. Hill thought

he saw an opening, made his move and was forced to brake hard to avoid contact. He lost it, but retained third place in the race and with it third place in championship. Mechanical failure took its toll as Schumacher retired on lap 20 due to engine failure and Hakkinen retired with brake pipe failure.

Senna achieved his 41st triumph, in his 158th race. It established McLaren as the most successful team in F1 history with 104 wins. The perfect end to the six year partnership. After the race Senna was visibly emotional and asked about his departure from McLaren said, "The records speak for themselves.

I leave friends behind and I think that's the best way to go." Prost was more restrained. Asked about the race he sai, "I would have loved to have won. I think I did a good race and can't complain about the traffic. I am happy to finish with a good race." And about the future? "It is not easy to say what is going to be my life in the future. But I am happy to change and maybe I will be much much happier, or maybe not. For sure my life will be different." Hand shakes and half embraces in the pit-lane and on the podium between Senna and Prost may not indicate a reconciliation, but the display is evidence of a deep mutual respect.

Charlie Whiting if FISA's F1 Technical Delegate. It is his job to ensure that all cars comply with regulations and he is first port of call if the teams require clarification of the regulations. Before joining FISA Whiting was Chief Mechanic at Brabham during its heyday.

"My role first and foremost is to ensure that the rules are applied in the same way in every country. Before there was a permanent technical delegate, different interpretations of rules existed in various different countries, so it was difficult for teams to know how to bring their cars along. I personally suffered that at Brabham. Secondly, it is to ensure that the cars are safe before they ever reach a GP. I attend the crash testing of chassis during the winter break, but I also supervise the structure tests that have to be done to every single chassis. I'm probably busier in the winter than during the season. During this time there is a lot of liaising with teams. If they have a query over a regulation and I clarify that, then I mean "Yes" for all of the races. As for the races themselves, the checks fall into two distinct categories.

On Thursday scrutineering takes place and with the help of local scrutineers we check 38 points relating to safety. We check that the cars are safe to go out on the track, but anything relating to performance is not necessarily checked on Thursday as wing heights etc. can be changed at a moments notice, so there is no point in picking somebody up on a rear wing that is a couple of millemeters too high. In our opinion it's when it comes off the track that that counts. We also take random fuel samples - five or ten· minutes before the car goes out for qualifying, when somebody will be waiting in the garage ready to take a sample, or directly after practice, but that is a little meaningless really because if anybody was cheating with the fuel they would not have it in at the end of practice.

During official qualifying we stop the cars on a random basis. We have the power to stop any car at any time, but a computer programme chooses the fourth car as it enters pit lane. If the car is chosen it will be confronted by a red light as it enters the pit lane and must undergo a series of checks. We systematically weigh the car, then check the front and rear wings, bodywork height and front and rear overhangs. The flat bottom is checked when the car is up on the scales. Sometimes we check that the driver's head is below the theoretical line between the two roll structures. Of course, we don't check the same things every time, because the teams would soon get wise to that.

At the end of the race the regulations require that all classified cars are weighed without the driver and before the end of the race a team manager, chosen at random by the stewards, will choose four cars out of a hat to undergo a complete scrutineering. We may verify that the fuel sample is coming from the tank the team say it is coming from and we ask the team to open the tank. Sometimes we check the fuel tank itself. We might go as far as checking the engine capacity.

There are many clever engineers and designers in the pit lane, hundreds of them and I'm only one. It is very difficult indeed to keep up with the current level of technology and to fully understand what might be going on.

There is far more to look at on a Williams, McLaren, Benetton than on a Lola. With high technology devices we have to be sure of what they do, in case there is a secondary purpose.

Ultimately, we have to rely on the teams to tell us what it does. If I see anything that I'm not sure of I ask the team "What does it do?" If we're not happy with the explanation we take it further.

For example, on active suspension we could possibly remove the computer from the car and have experts download the software. It may be unrealistic, but we

could do that if we wanted to. I think the designers respect the fact that I have a job to do and that job is only to make sure that they are playing the game and that the playing field is level.

There are some cynical people about who believe that manipulation happens to try to improve the show, but that is simply not true.

I have a good relationship with all the teams, but sometimes the job involves making tough decisions which are not universally popular, as in Canada…"

FINISHING ORDER			
DRIVER	CAR	AVERAGE	DELAY
1. **Ayrton Senna**	McLaren	173.183	-
2. **Alain Prost**	Williams	172.926	9.258
3. **Damon Hill**	Williams	172.243	33.902
4. **Jean Alesi**	Ferrari	170.976	1 lap
5. **Gerhard Berger**	Ferrari	170.964	1 lap
6. **Martin Brundle**	Ligier	169.455	1 lap
7. **Aguri Suzuki**	Footwork	169.095	1 lap
8. **Riccardo Patrese**	Benetton	169.089	2 laps
9. **Mark Blundell**	Ligier	167.731	2 laps
10. **Derek Warwick**	Footwork	167.010	2 laps
11. **Rubens Barrichello**	Jordan	165.240	3 laps
12. **Erik Comas**	Larrousse	165.221	3 laps
13. **Andrea De Cesaris**	Tyrrell	162.635	4 laps
14. **Toshio Suzuki**	Larrousse	160.212	5 laps
15. **Karl Wendlinger**	Sauber	169.113	6 laps

RETIREMENTS			
DRIVER	CAR	LAPS	REASON
Pedro Lamy	Lotus	1	Accident
Pierluigi Martini	Minardi	5	Gear
Jonny Herbert	Lotus	9	Suspension
Eddie Irvine	Jordan	10	Accident
Ukyo Katayama	Tyrrell	11	Suspension
Michael Schumacher	Benetton	19	Engine
Mika Hakkinen	McLaren	28	Breaks
Jean Mark Gounon	Minardi	34	About-face
J.J. Lehto	Sauber	56	Accident

BEST LAPS			
DRIVER	LAP	TIME	AVE.
Hill	64	1'15"381	180.523
Prost	66	1'15"434	180.396
Senna	70	1'16"128	178.752
Berger	74	1'16"686	177.451
Schumacher	17	1'17"069	176.569
Patrese	67	1'17"478	175.637
Brundle	63	1'17"565	175.440
Alesi	40	1'17"786	174.942
Wendlinger	50	1'18"101	174.236
Blundell	53	1'18"314	173.762
A. Suzuki	49	1'18"316	173.758
Lehto	49	1'18"430	173.505
Barrichello	53	1'18"558	173.222
Warwick	55	1'18"905	172.461
Hakkinen	17	1'18"960	172.340
Comas	76	1'19"152	171.922
Herbert	8	1'20"502	169.039
De Cesaris	36	1'20"625	168.781
Martini	5	1'21"175	167.638
Gounon	34	1'21"678	166.605
Irvine	9	1'21"742	166.745
Katayama	5	1'22"143	165.662
T. Suzuki	52	1'22"328	165.290

▼ *In a symbolic gesture on the victory podium Senna and Prost forget their differences and finally acknowledge their mutual respect for one another's talents. The 3rd player, Damon Hill, will have to come to terms with Senna's skill as they become teammates at Williams for 1994.*

KYALAMI

La speranza di Damon Hill di un
debutto da sogno per la squadra
delle Canon Williams è sfumata
con un'uscita sulle sabbie del
Westbank, causata dalla manovra
di sorpasso di Alessandro Zanardi.

*Damon Hill's hope of a dream
debut for the Canon Williams
Team ended in the sandtrap at
Westbank following Alessandro
Zanardi's optimistic overtaking
manouvre.*

KYALAMI

Riccardo Patrese, il campione più
anziano delle corse di Gran
Premio ha rinnovato la sua sfida
correndo in coppia sulla Benetton
con il dinamico giovane astro
Michael Schumacher.
(Nella pagina seguente)

*Riccardo Patrese, the elder
statesman of Grand Prix racing
took on a new challenge at
Benetton partnering the
dynamic young star Michael
Schumacher.*
(Following page)

KYALAMI

La scelta di Minardi di passare ai motori Ford ha portato risultati immediati alla piccola squadra italiana. Il piazzamento al quarto posto di Christian Fittipaldi a Kyalami ha dissipato tutti i dubbi, dimostrando la sorprendente capacità della Minardi di competere anche con i giganti della Formula Uno.

Minardi's move to Ford power brought immediate results for the small Italian equipe. Christian Fittipaldi's fourth position at Kyalami eclipsed all expectations in the face of stern opposition from the bigger and better financed giants of Formula One.

KYALAMI

Il rientro di Gerhard Berger alla Ferrari, la casa spiritualmente a lui più congeniale, è salutato con favore da tutti i suoi sostenitori italiani.
(Nella pagina accanto)

The return of Gerhard Berger to Ferrari, his spiritual home, was welcomed by all supporters of the great Italian team.
(Opposite)

KYALAMI

Il ritorno alla ribalta della Lotus continua alla direzione di Peter Collins; qui il suo giovane protetto Johnny Herbert e Alessandro Zanardi mostrano il loro talento alla guida delle multicolori (e multifinanziate) vetture di Formula Uno.
(Nella pagina seguente)

The return to prominence of Team Lotus continues in the hands of Peter Collins, here his young proteges, Johnny Herbert and Alessandro Zanardi display their talents in the multicoloured and multisponsored F1 cars.
(Following page)

KYALAMI

Alain Prost ha diradato ogni dubbio circa il suo impegno e il rendimento dopo un intero anno di riposo, ottenendo al suo rientro un'abilissima e schiacciante vittoria.

Alain Prost dispelled any doubts about his commitment and pace after his year long sabbatical with a masterful and dominant victory on his return.

KYALAMI

Lo sfortunato Ivan Capelli si è unito alla squadra di Eddi Jourdan sperando che la sorte potesse volgere al meglio; il verdetto non si è fatto attendere a lungo.
(In alto a sinistra)

The luckless Ivan Capelli joined Eddie Jordan's team hoping that his fortunes might change for the better, he didn't have to wait long for the answer.
(Above right)

INTERLAGOS

Contro tutti i pronostici, Ayrton Senna ricambia il tifo spasmodico dei suoi compatrioti, con una vittoria sbalorditiva nel Gran Premio brasiliano. Ron Dennis vive il momento al massimo dell'entusiasmo.
(Nella pagina seguente)

Against all odds, Ayrton Senna satisfied his compatriots wild fervour with a stunning victory at his home Grand Prix, Ron Dennis makes the most of the moment.
(Following page)

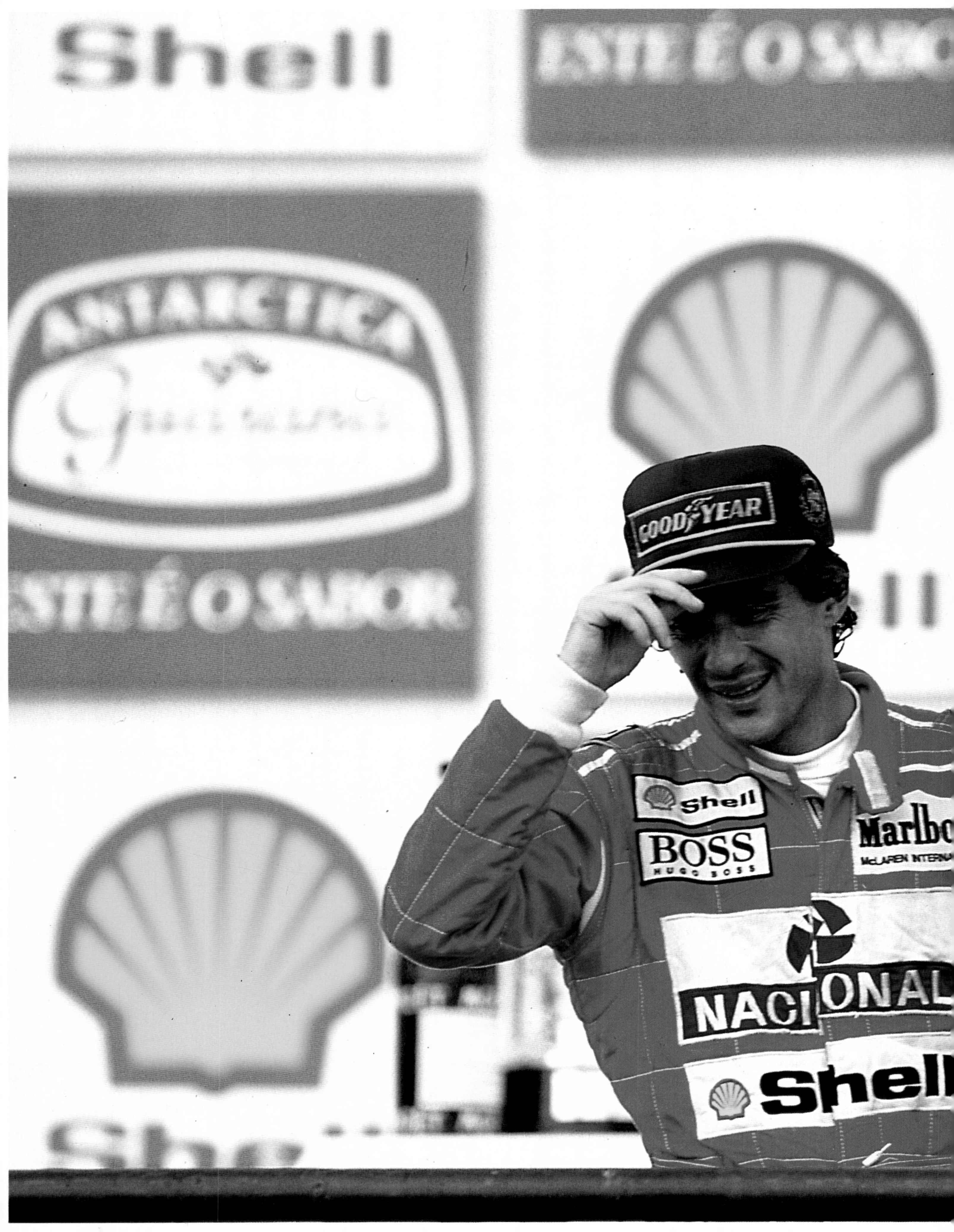
Shell
ANTARCTICA
GOODYEAR
Shell
BOSS
HUGO BOSS
Shell

DONINGTON

Che la gara sostenuta da Ayrton Senna a Donington sia stata fra le sue migliori prestazioni è discutibile: senz'altro gran parte delle difficoltà incontrate su questo circuito sono dovute alle condizioni sempre variabili dell'instabile clima britannico.

Ayrton Senna celebrates arguably his greatest ever drive in the ever changing conditions provided by the great British weather.

DONINGTON

Alain Prost e Damon Hill seguono la scia dell'abilissimo brasiliano, lungo la svolta del Redgate del Parco di Donington.
(Nella pagina seguente)

Alain Prost and Damon Hill trail the masterful Brazilian through Redgate corner at Donington Park.
(Following page)

DONINGTON

Appena al suo terzo Gran Premio Rubens Barrichello ha sbalordito l'opinione pubblica dimostrando grande abilità; qui sfida Berger per l'ottava posizione alla partenza.

In only his third Grand Prix, Rubens Barrichello stunned the establishement with his maturity and speed, here he challenges Berger for eighth at the start.

DONINGTON

Il proprietario del circuito, Tom Weathcroft, realizza l'ambizione di tutta la sua vita facendo tornare le macchine del Gran Premio a Donington Park. Senna riceve i premi per la vittoria sul circuito che ha visto il suo debutto in F1.
(In alto a destra)

Circuit owner Tom Wheatcroft realises his life-long ambition with the return of Grand Prix cars to Donington Park. Senna accepts the spoils of victory at the circuit where he made his F1 debut.
(Above right)

Therry Boutsen si è unito alla squadra della Jordan sostituendo tardivamente Ivan Capelli; qui sta passando vicino allo Spitfire dell'ultima guerra mondiale, permanentemente in mostra a Donington.

Therry Boutsen joined the Jordan team as a late replacement for Ivan Capelli, here he passes the World War Two spitfire which is a permanent exhibit at Donington.

DONINGTON

Rubens Barrichello si dimostra
sorprendentemente preparato ad
affrontare le difficili condizioni
atmosferiche di Donington. Il
giovane brasiliano ha corso
sempre dietro al suo eroe e
connazionale Ayrton Senna.
Soltanto a causa di problemi con
la pressione dell'olio non ha
potuto condividere il podio col
vincitore della corsa.
(Nella pagina precedente)

*Rubens Barrichello copes
admirably with the apalling
conditions at Donington. The
young brazialian ran second to
his hero and fellow countryman
Senna. Only fuel pressure
problems robbed him of sharing
the podium with the race winner.*
(Preceding page)

IMOLA

Philippe Alliot, al segnale del via
fa rombare vigorosamente il
motore Lamborghini V12 della
sua F.1; finirà poi con un
incoraggiante quinto
piazzamento, conquistando alla
squadra i primi punti della
stagione.

*Philippe Alliot gives the signal
to start the glorious sounding
Lamborghini V12 in his
Larrouse F1, he later finished
an encouraging fifth, scoring
the teams first points of the
year.*

IMOLA

L' avvilente inizio di stagione di Andretti si è prolungato con un imbarazzante testacoda fuori dall'ultima chicane, davanti ai box: la macchina si è schiantata contro il muro di fronte. Più tardi nel pomeriggio il compagno di squadra, Senna, ha ripetuto il testacoda finendo però a pochi centimetri dal muro dei box.

Andretti's miserable start to the season continued with an embarassing spin out of the last chicane in front of the pits, the car slamming into the pit wall. Later in the afternoon team mate Senna repeated the spin but finished mere centimetres from the pit wall.

IMOLA

Nella pagina accanto:
Opposite:

Barrichello non è riuscito a ripetere la prova di Donington; malgrado le condizioni fossero simili, non è giunto all'arrivo.

Barrichello could not repeat the showing at Donington despite similar conditions, he failed to finish.

Berger riflette sulla strategia di gara da adottare per soddisfare gli ansiosi tifosi di Imola.

Berger contemplates his strategy before endeavouring to satisfy the expectant tifosi at Imola.

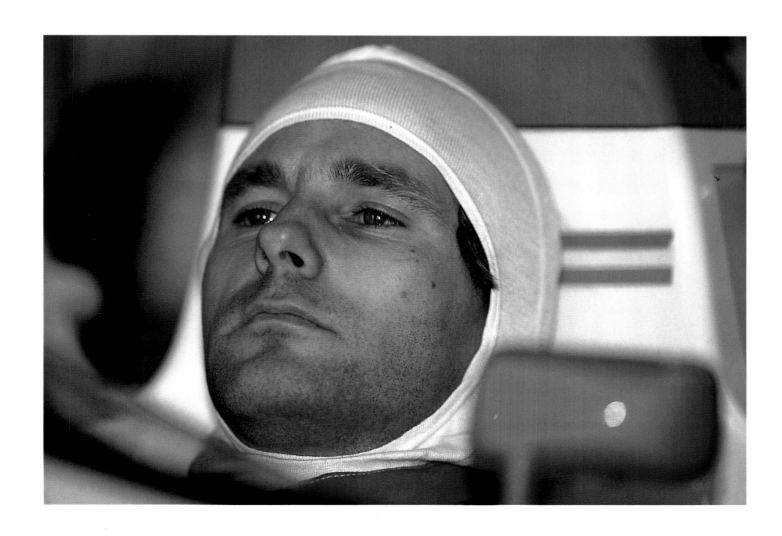

CATALUNYA

Nelle pagine precedenti:
Preceding pages:

Alla fine la fortuna ha arriso a
Michael Andretti, facendogli
registrare il risultato di gran lunga
migliore della stagione, con un
incoraggiante quinto posto.

*Michael Andretti's luck finally
changed, the charging American
scoring by far his best result of
the season with a confidence
boosting fith place.*

La superiore potenza delle
Williams Renault ha strappato
ancora una volta il primo posto
sul podio a Michael Schumacher.
Sia Senna sia Schumacher hanno
lottato per le posizioni restanti,
nella classe dei motori Ford.

*The superior power of the
Williams Renaults once again
kept Michael Schumacher from
the premiere position on the
podium, both Senna and
Schumacher fought for honours
behind in the Ford engined
class.*

CATALUNYA

La vittoria ha aiutato il francese
Prost a guadagnare terreno per
assicurarsi il titolo del campionato
piloti per la quarta volta.

*Prost's victory helped the
Frenchman gather momentum
in his bid to secure the drivers
championship for the fourth
time.*

CATALUNYA

Blundell fa un cenno a Warwick che potrebbe iniziare la contesa; malgrado la rivalità in pista, i due piloti sono ottimi amici e nutrono grande stima reciproca.

Blundell indicates to Warwick that battle may commence, despite their rivalry on the track, both drivers are the best of friends and have great respect for each other.

CATALUNYA

Damon Hill insegue l'inafferrabile prima vittoria con una partenza travolgente nella prima serie di curve a Barcellona.

Damon Hill chases that elusive first victory by making a storming start into the first series of bends at Barcelona.

CATALUNYA

Boutsen fissa intensamente il monitor prima di uscire per il giro di qualificazione al Gran Premio di Spagna, a Barcellona.
(Nella pagina accanto)

Boutsen stares into the timing monitor before setting off on his qualifying lap for the Spanish Grand Prix in Barcelona.
(Opposite)

CATALUNYA

Ukyo Katayama, il pilota
proveniente dalla Larrousse, è
entrato all'inizio della stagione
nella Tyrrell Yamaha, team di cui
appare visibilmente soddisfatto.

*Ukyo Katayama, the Tyrrell
Yamaha driver who joined the
team from Larrouse at the start
of the season reflects on the
joys of being a Tyrrell driver.*

MONACO

Jean Alesi, il re della velocità, ha intrattenuto il meraviglioso pubblico di Monaco con un'ulteriore brillante dimostrazione di abilità di guida, assicurarando un prezioso terzo posto alla Ferrari.

Jean Alesi, the king of speed entertained the beautiful people of Monaco with yet another flamboyant diplay of driving skills on his way to a much needed third place for Ferrari.

MONACO

Zanardi spinge fuori pista la sua Lotus sponsorizzata da Castrol, durante le qualificazioni per il Gran Premio di Monaco.
(Nella pagina accanto)

Zanardi pushes his Castrol sponsored Lotus over the kerbs during qualifying for the Monaco G.P.
(Opposite)

MONACO

Ayrton Senna, mister Monaco dei nostri giorni, conduce la sua McLaren attraverso piazza Casinò. Non del tutto riavutosi dall'impatto ad alta velocità contro le barriere di St. Devot, Senna ha dimostrato di essere ancora il protagonista sulle strade del Principato.

Ayrton Senna, the modern day Mr. Monaco guides his Marlboro McLaren through Casino square. Despite not being fully recovered from his high speed encounter with the barriers at St Devot, Senna proved yet again that he is the master in the streets of the principality.

MONACO

Il crollo di Alain Prost al Gran Premio di Monaco è imputabile ai problemi che si sono verificati alla frizione. Prost ha riportato una penalità di 10 secondi in seguito a una falsa partenza ed è andato in panne ai box durante il rientro in gara, perdendo così le possibilità di un'altra vittoria a Monaco.
(Nella pagina seguente)

Clutch problems were the downfall of Alain Prosts Monaco Grand Prix. Prost suffered a 10 second penalty as a result of a jump start, and stalled in the pits when rejoining the race, thus eliminating his chances of yet another Monaco victory.
(Following page)

MONACO

Damon Hill, tentando di emulare
il record di vittorie di suo padre,
famoso pilota ora scomparso, ha
sfiorato la sua prima vittoria sulle
pittoresche strade di Monaco.
L'intervento della Ferrari di
Berger al Loews per poco non lo
ha costretto concludere in quel
punto la corsa: la peggio
nell'incidente è toccata al pilota
austriaco.

*Damon Hill's efforts to emulate
his late great father's Monaco
record of wins almost succeeded
with a first win on the
picturesque streets of Monaco.
The intervention of Bergers
Ferrari at Loews almost ended
his race there, but Berger came
off worse in the incident.*

MONACO

Eddie Jourdan festeggia a
Monaco il ventunesimo
compleanno di Rubens
Barrichello; il dirigente della
squadra è soddisfatto delle
notevoli prestazioni d'inizio
stagione del suo nuovo pilota.

*Eddie Jordan celebrates Rubens
Barrichello's 21st birthday at
Monaco, the team owner
delighted with his new driver
and impressive performance to
the start of the season.*

MONACO

Dereck Warwick si impegna a
fondo per attraversare il tunnel di
Monaco: su questo tratto si
raggiungono velocità anche di
290 chilometri orari, spesso con i
concorrenti a distanza ravvicinata.

*Dereck Warwick shows the
commitment required when
negotiating the tunnel in
Monaco at speeds of up to 180
mph with fellow competitors
following close behind.*

MONTREAL

Nella pagina accanto:
Opposite:

Senna scova un angolo tranquillo
e isolato nei box McLaren, prima
dell'inizio della gara; in seguito
subentrerà il disappunto, dopo
una agguerrita battaglia con Alesi
durante i giri d'apertura.

*Senna finds a quiet and
secluded corner in the McLaren
pit garage before the start of the
race, dissapointment was to
follow after a titanic battle with
Alesi during the opening laps.*

Gerhard Berger sulla scia di
quanto realizzato dal suo
compagno di squadra a Monte
Carlo, è finito al quarto posto con
un altro entusiasmante
avanzamento in zona punti. Qui
precede la Ligier di Brundle.

*Gerhard Berger continued the
trend started by his team mate
in Monte Carlo by finishing
fourth with another stirring
drive into the points, here he
leads Brundles Ligier.*

MONTREAL

Le Williams si trovano ancora in testa nella prima curva del circuito Gilles Villeneuve, ma le due Ferrari conducono l'inseguimento preludendo al finale ribaltamento dei piazzamenti.

The Williams' lead yet again into the first corner at the circuit Gilles Villeneuve, both Ferraris lead the chase indicating an upturn in fortunes at last for the Scuderia.

MONTREAL

Johnny Herbert attende
pazientemente nell'abitacolo della
sua Lotus prima di avventurarsi al
confronto con i franco-canadesi,
entusiasti e preparatissimi.

*Johnny Herbert waits patently
in the cockpit of his Lotus
before venturing out in front of
the enthusiastic and
knowledgable French-
Canadians.*

MONTREAL

Alain Prost, ancora una volta
irraggiungibile dopo aver
sorpassato Hill, ha guadagnato
altri 10 punti per la vittoria in
campionato, mentre il suo astuto
rivale Senna, ha dovuto
interrompere la gara.
(Nella pagina seguente)

*Alain Prost was again
unstoppable once past Hill. He
fuelled his Championship
aspirations with another ten
points when his arch rival
Senna failed to finish.*
(Following page)

MONTREAL

Mark Blundell studia il monitor
della Olivetti durante le
qualificazioni; questi rivelatori
sono fondamentali, perchè sono
in grado di dare ai piloti i tempi di
ciascun giro, non appena le auto
passano il traguardo nel corso
delle qualificazioni.

*Mark Blundell studies the
Olivetti timing monitor during
qualifying, these monitors are
invaluable during the weekend
showing every driver the lap
times as the cars cross the line
during qualifying.*

MONTREAL

Damon Hill accelera lungo il
circuito Gilles Villeneuve;
all'orizzonte, lo spettacolare
scenario del cielo di Montreal.

*Damon Hill speeds past on the
circuit Gilles Villeneuve with the
Montreal skyline as a
spectacular backdrop.*

MAGNY-COURS

Nella pagina accanto:
Opposite:

Alla partenza del Gran Premio di
Francia Damon Hill prende il
comando alla prima curva dalla
pole-position; durante la corsa è
stato costretto a cedere il
comando a uno scatenato Prost,
che si è immediatamente
aggiudicato la vittoria del Gran
Premio francese.

*The start of the French Grand
Prix saw Damon Hill lead into
the first corner from pole
position, he was later to
relinquish his lead to a charging
Prost who stormed through to
victory at his home Grand Prix.*

Le Footwork gemelle di Aguri
Suzuki e di Derek Warwick
corrono vicine durante le fasi
conclusive del Gran Premio di
Francia.

*The Footwork twins of Aguri
Suzuki and Derek Warwick lap
together during the closing
stages of the French Grand
Prix.*

MAGNY-COURS

Il circuito di Magny Cours offre pittoresche panoramiche di sfondo al Gran Premio di Francia; qui Hill conduce davanti a Senna e Patrese alla curva di Adelaide. Jean Alesi, particolarmente caricato per quest'appuntamento, ancora una volta ha avuto problemi con la Ferrari; Prost e Hill hanno così celebrato la vittoria.

The Magny Cours circuit provides some picturesque backgrounds to the French Grand Prix, here Hill leads Senna and Patrese at Adelaide corner. Jean Alesi was also in spectacular mood during the weekend but once again suffered at the hands of the Ferrari, Prost and Hill celebrate.

MAGNY-COURS

Alessandro Zanardi, su Castrol Lotus, si concede una pausa durante le prove di sabato delle qualificazioni finali.
(Nella pagina seguente)

Alessandro Zanardi of Castrol Lotus takes a break from qualifying during Saturday final qualifying.
(Following page)

MAGNY-COURS

Il sabato, Martin Brundle, della francese Ligier, e il suo compagno di squadra Mark Blundell hanno dato ai sostenitori della casa francese un ottimo motivo per cui rallegrarsi piazzando le due Ligier in seconda fila. Qui Brundle si concentra prima dell'uscita finale in pista per le qualificazioni.

Martin Brundle in the French Ligier equipe, and team mate Mark Blundell gave the home supporters plenty to cheer about by placing the two Ligiers on the second row, Brundle here concentrates before his final sortie onto the track for qualifying.

MAGNY-COURS

Venerdì, Karl Wendlinger discute con il team manager Peter Sauber durante la sessione di prove. Purtroppo l'austriaco non ha avuto fortuna e non ha guadagnato punti dopo il promettente inizio di stagione. *(Foto nel riquadro)*

Karl Wendlinger confers with team principal Peter Sauber during the Friday practice session, the Austrian was unfortunately out of luck and did not finish in the points after the promising start to the season.
(Small picture)

SILVERSTONE

Il 249° Gran Premio di Riccardo
Patrese ha segnato una svolta in
una stagione cominciata in
maniera difficile. Il Gran Premio
di Gran Bretagna lo ha visto
infatti ritornare sul podio,
traguardo per lui abituale finchè è
rimasto alla guida delle Williams.
(Nella pagina seguente)

*Riccardo Patrese's 249th Grand
Prix marked a turning point in
what had started out as a
difficult season. The British
Grand Prix saw him return to
the podium, a regular occurence
during his Williams days.*
(Following page)

SILVERSTONE

Le straordinarie condizioni di
forma che la Sauber ha sfoggiato
all'inizio della stagione
sfortunatamente non si sono
riviste durante il fine settimana del
Gran Premio di Gran Bretagna.
La squadra, tuttavia, ha
continuato a lavorare assiduamente per migliorarne le
prestazioni in vista dell'ultima
parte della stagione.

*The tremendous form shown at
the beginning of the season by
Sauber was unfortunately not
reproduced during the British
Grand Prix weekend, the team
however were working hard on
developments for the latter part
of the season.*

SILVERSTONE

Il tifo della folla di spettatori radunatisi a Silverstone ha spronato tutti i piloti britannici a dare il meglio di sè. In particolare Derek Warwick si è coraggiosamente lanciato in una competizione frenetica con Alesi e Blundell per conquistare la zona punti.

The support shown by the Silverstone crowd brought out the very best in all the British drivers especially the ever cheerful Derek Warwick. He battled courageously with Alesi and Blundell during a frantic race to finish in the points.

SILVERSTONE

Damon Hill conduce gran parte del Gran Premio di Gran Bretagna davanti a Prost; il giovane inglese, esaltato per l'occasione, ha affrontato la gara in modo ammirevole, finché un problema meccanico non gli ha impedito di vincere il suo primo Gran Premio. Prost ha preso il comando e lo ha mantenuto fino alla vittoria, conquistando altri punti per il campionato.

Damon Hill leads Prost during the British Grand Prix, the young Brit was certainly fired up for the occasion and performed admirably until a mechanical problem robbed him of his first Grand Prix win. Prost however took over the lead and cruised to another victory and more championship points.

HOCKENHEIM

Damon Hill entra davanti a
Schumacher nel circuito di
Hockenheim; la folla tedesca ha
acclamato con entusiasmo
Schumacher e gli ha dato tutto il
sostegno possibile e perfino più
del dovuto. Il pilota tedesco ha
ripagato i suoi sostenitori con una
tra le prestazioni più
sorprendenti.

*Damon Hill leads Schumacher
into the Hockenheim stadium,
the German crowd went wild
giving Schumaker all the
support and more that he
needed for his home Grand Prix
and he responded by giving one
of his most stunning drives.*

HOCKENHEIM

Dopo una intensa battaglia con
Gerhard Berger, tale che Nigel
Mansell ne sarebbe andato fiero,
il britannico Mark Blundell ha
uguagliato il suo miglior risultato
in un Gran Premio con un terzo
posto assai meritato.

*After a fraught battle with
Gerhard Berger, the likes of
which Nigel Mansell would be
proud, Briton Mark Blundell
equalled his best ever Grand
Prix result with a hard earned
and richly deserved third place.*

HOCKENHEIM

Schumacher saluta la folla dopo
un superbo secondo piazzamento;
il fervore patriottico senza dubbio
lo ha aiutato nell'impresa; chissà
che cosa ci si potrebbe aspettare
dalla folla il giorno in cui
Schumacher dovesse vincere ad
Hockenheim!

*Schumacher salutes the crowd
after a superb second, the
patriotic fervour undoubtedly
helped him on his way, if he
ever wins at Hockenheim
heaven knows what to expect
from the crowd.*

HOCKENHEIM

La cattiva sorte di Damon Hill lo ha perseguitato anche a Hockenheim; pochi avrebbero supposto che la vittoria gli sarebbe stata così bruscamente strappata dalle mani, a un solo giro dall'arrivo. I team managers della squadra, Frank Williams e Patrick Head, fotografati con Damon durante il sabato delle qualificazioni.

Damon Hill's run of bad luck continued at Hockenheim, few would have beleived that victory was so cruelly snatched from his grasp only a lap from home, here he flashes past the capacity filled stadium before his demise. Team principals Frank Williams and Patrick head are seen with Damon during qualifying on Saturday.

HOCKENHEIM

Gerhard Berger ancora una volta ha dato il meglio di sé durante il fine settimana: il culmine della sua prestazione si è avuto la domenica, quando ha sostenuto una esaltante sfida con la Ligier di Mark Blundell.

Gerhard Berger once again gave his all throughout the weekend, culminating in a gritty drive on the Sunday, the highlight being his battle with the Ligier of Mark Blundell.

HOCKENHEIM

La Sasol Jordan di Thierry
Boutsen, durante le qualificazioni,
solleva una ruota alla terza
chicane di Hockenheim; il belga,
che ha corso per il decimo anno
in Formula Uno, è stato incapace
di uguagliare i risultati conseguiti
in precedenza durante la sua
carriera.

*The Sasol Jordan of Thierry
Boutsen lifts a wheel during
qualifying at the third chicane
at Hockenheim, the Belgian
racing in his tenth year of
Formula One unable to equal
the results previously gained
during his career.*

HOCKENHEIM

Mentre Michael Schumacher, ex
compagno di squadra nel gruppo
Mercedes, gli ha rubato ancora
una volta le luci della ribalta,
l'austriaco Karl Wendlinger ha
continuato a perfezionare la
vettura di Formula Uno della
Sauber.

*While Karl Wendlingers ex
team mate in the Mercedes
Group C. Team, Michael
Schumacher one again stole the
limelight, the Austrian
continued the development of
the Sauber F1 machine.*

TECHNICAL NEWS - GOODYEAR, BARRY GRIFFIN - TYRE CHANGES '93

In 1993 FISA imposed new tyre regulations and in so doing posed a design challenge to Goodyear, the sole supplier of tyres in Formula 1. Under the rules the maximum height of a rear tyre is 26" and the width, when fitted and inflated on a wheel, must not exceed 15". The knock-on effect was that not only did a new rear tyre have to be developed, but a new front tyre too, to maintain the balance of the car's handling between the front and the rear. Barry Griffin, Manager of International Racing Public Relations, spoke on behalf of Goodyear about how that challenge was met and the impact the change in regulations has had on the ground this season.

"When we were told about the regulations, our engineers looked at them and made the decision whether we could make a safe and competitive tyre. The thing that is paramount to Goodyear in racing is safety. We are in it for our image and if we have tyres that are not performing well, then we might as well not be here. If we have cars flying and sliding off into the barriers or drivers and spectators being hurt, that is not the image Goodyear wants. We looked at our sums. Three inches were lost on the rear tyre, which represents 17% of the footprint of each rear tyre. That was a considerable loss, so we were apprehensive about having to give up that amount, but Goodyear never contested it." The loss of footprint was not the only concern. In order for a tyre to sustain the load upon it, it must contain a certain amount of air. Griffin describes air as "the life support system of a tyre. Without it it will collapse." In Formula 1 the load is not just the weight of the engine and the chassis. The downforce created by aerodynamic aids can increase the weight of the car by possibly a factor of four. As Griffin explained, "Had we been concerned that the extra load on the smaller tyre was impinging into the Goodyear self-imposed safety limits, then we would have gone back to FISA and said "This is not a good idea. We are getting into the realms where a tyre of that dimension cannot sustain those loads at the speeds reached." However, the maths of the situation said a tyre of those dimensions was capable of doing it."

A racing tyre is designed for one specific job, which never lasts more than two hours. At the end of that it is thrown away as scrap. The tyre has to withstand not only high speed and load, but also high temperatures, sometimes as high as 140F. It is necessary to ensure that the construction of a tyre can withstand the heat that will be produced in any one race. Control of the heat can be achieved in various ways, principally by the thickness of the tread rubber. Grip, a primary requirement, is achieved by the construction of the bulk material underneath and the carcass. As for details, "Those are trade secrets!", said Griffin.

Did redesign for 1993 pose Goodyear a problem? "Not a problem,

Professor Syd Watkins has been an integral part of Grand Prix racing for many years. He is a likeable and jovial gentleman who attends each and every Grand Prix. Without him and his rapid life saving actions several drivers throughout the years would not be here with us today, the most recent being that of Martin Donnelly saved by Prof at the 1991 Spanish Grand Prix at Jerez.

Charlie Whiting is now the man responsible for the formulation of the technical regulations in Formula One, this year in Canada he was the centre of attention after ruling that almost all the cars competing in Formula One were illegal, thus enforcing a change in the regulations for the 1994 F1 season. He is an ex Brabham mechanic from the days when Bernie Ecclestone was team owner at the Chessington based equipe.

These days each team use electrically insulated tyre warmers to heat the tyres before they are fitted to the F1 car.

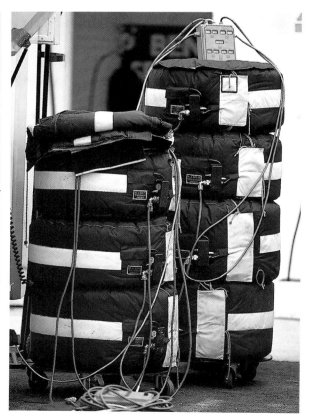

but a challenge." said Griffin, " We have wealth of experience in categories other than GP racing, particularly in America, where they race relatively small tyres with high speed and heavy loads. A point in case is NASCAR on the ovals, where the tyres are relatively small. In Indycars they race under tyre restrictions as well, so Goodyear have a lot of experience of making tyres with small physical dimensions that have to perform very competitively. We were able to draw on our American experience and incorporate it into F1 technology."

Goodyear was told about the change in regulations in August 1992 and tested the first of the new tyres the week after Estoril. "We did a weeks testing there and the results were very encouraging. From day one it was apparent that we were very close to having our tyre life."

Goodyear recognised many years ago that it could not operate by making a tyre for each team,

but worked towards having the best compromise tyre available to all. "We work closely with the teams. Experience shows that if you have a tyre that works on a Williams, McLaren, Ferrari or Benetton, it will also work on a Tyrell or a Footwork as well. When we go testing, we never test with one team. We like three teams there and we might, say, test a new front tyre with McLaren and a new rear tyre with Williams. Then we'd swop them around, then put the two together and then we'd ask both teams to compare each others choices, so that we arrive at the best common denominator", said Griffin.

Goodyear supplies all 26 teams and to do this about 2,000 tyres are taken to each Grand Prix, of which about 600 are rain tyres and the rest made up of usually two dry compounds. Griffin explained that "Experience tells us what compound

will suit a particular circuit. That will be our "prime tyre" and we will take a few tyres of a harder compound, just in case." There are occasions, such as Monza and Monaco, when Goodyear will attend with only one compound.

This season each team has been limited to seven sets of tyres per driver, per event. Those teams that pay to use the tyres pay $600 (US) per tyre. It is a

service fee payable to Goodyear and the teams do not own the tyres. For that $600 the tyre is made, shipped to whichever location required and is serviced by Goodyear. Griffin maintains that "While $600 sounds a lot of

Goodyear technicians balance each and every tyre/wheel before they are returned to their respective teams for practice, qualifying and race.

This shows the difference in size between the 1992 Goodyear tyres and the 1993 F1 racing tyre.

money, the teams generally think that it represents good value for what they get."

The visible difference between this year's tyre and last year's is size, but what else is different? Griffin said that whilst the same range of compounds is being use for the smaller tyres, "We are having to race one compound harder on each track than we did last year. If we raced Bs last year, we are racing As this year. Last year at Monaco we raced the D tyre, this year we used the C tyre. The other affect on the tyres is that we are using increased tyre pressures, an extra 2 psi all round, and the tyre temperatures have increased. Smaller tyre, increased relative load, working har-

der, therefore getting warmer." And the impact of the change in the regulations on F1 itself? At Estoril, a tortious track where grip is vital and tyres central to the performance of any chassis, this season Prost's pole position time was a second under Mansell's at Estoril in 1992. Draw your own conclusions.

ACTIVE SUSPENSION - THE END OF AN ERA

Team Lotus has long been associated with innovative design and deve- lopment. Lotus decided to build a road car using active suspension before embarking on a full racing programme, due to the novel nature of the technology. It took six months to build an active Lotus Esprit and a further six months to develop the car. When Colin Chapman was taken round Snetterton by Elio de Angelis he immediately recognised the potential of the system and gave the go ahead to build a racing version. On 16th December 1982 Peter Wright, Lotus Technical Director, was at Snetterton for the first run of the racing version when he was told of Champman's death the night before. Wright has been at the heart of the development of active suspension, working with both Team Lotus and Lotus Engineering.

Where did it all begin?

"The story really starts back when the 88 twin chassis car was banned. We had already been thinking of active suspension as a result of our association with Cranfield. We'd been talking about active suspension and when the 88 was banned, we said, "OK, plan A is not allowed, let's try plan B."

From 1983 to 1987 the system was not used in F1. Was the project shelved?

"At the end of '82 we had just got the F1 car running. The active car had been designed for skirtless ground effect cars and FISA changed the rules again, in came the flat bottom rules and the whole reason for doing it disappeared. I took the technology and the people working on it down to Lotus Engineering. In '87 Team Lotus knocked on our door, asking us to do a system for the F1 car. Flat bottom cars and aerodynamics had got to the stage where the cars needed active suspension."

What is active suspension all about?

"Ground effect is formed by the passage of air between the car and the road. The shape of the duct that the air passes through determines the pressure distribution and the amount of downforce. The problem is that ground effect works best when the gap at the front is 5-10mm and 20-50mm at the rear. It is very sensitive to those dimensions, so if the front goes down 2mm it has very different characteristics compared to being up at 15mm. The trouble is that if you brake a car at 4G and the car is mounted on springs - and one has to bear in mind that the tyres are springs themselves

- the front of the car goes down 10mm, so as you brake, the shape of the duct underneath changes radically and even worse if you go over bumps. As the aerodynamic loads increase on the car, the speed increases, the car squashes down onto the road, and the duct between the car and the road changes shape. With that change in shape, there is a change in aerodynamic characteristics. This change is always opposite to what you want. As the car brakes the front goes down and the gap at the front changes. Just when you need more downforce at the front, you get mo-

re at the rear. If you have active suspension you can push against that force. You add energy to the suspension system and hold the gap to what you want by raising the car as it brakes and shifting some load to the rear."

What individual items make up the system?

"The active suspension system is made up of sensors, computer and actuators. The best analogy to a fully active system is the human body, with its nerves as sensors, brain as computer and muscles as actuators. We don't use springs, but active suspension. The sensors measure load, position, and velocity. These sensors then feed the computer, where there is a set of equations, and the computer then sends a signal to the hydraulic valve, which sends hydraulic oil to either side of the pistons, which move the actuators. With each movement of the car everything changes and the system is set in motion

again at a rate of one thousand times a second. The software is the key. You can have this system and it will do absolutely nothing if the programme does not tell it to, as can sometimes be seen on the track!"

Now that the system has been outlawed, can the information and experience accumulated over recent years be applied to designing a passive car?

"Active suspension allows you to take out the compromises. Normally a passive system is very stiff, so the aerodynamic loads don't push the car into the road at high speed, but you want to run the car as low as possible at a low speed. The first thing that everyone has done with active suspension, whatever their system, is to run softer springs and

yet keep the cars off the road at high speed. So that is one of the compromises taken out. Working on the active suspension system has given us a foundation of knowledge of what all the parts of a suspension system do. We will be working very hard to come up with a passive suspension for whatever the regulations permit that takes out each of the compromises for a conventional passive system. How many we will take out remains to be seen. However, there is one compromise we will not be able to take out. We will not be able to modify the aerodynamics. That is the essence of FISA's decision. You cannot modify the aerodynamics by using anything other than a active system."

Technology in F1 is more advanced and the rules increasingly complex in the face of those advances. What are the difficulties of applying those rules?

"Twenty years ago you could take any part of a GP car and say "I know how it works". Take the key parts of a car today and people would ask for the part number. That's probably as far as they could go. You can't look

at a bit and say "I understand that". That's the problem with the technical rules. Nobody can figure out what they are doing and whether they meet the rules or not. Hardware can do any one of ten thousand different things, some of which are legal, some illegal. The rules have to attack not the hardware but the function. That is much harder to legislate for."

TELEMETRY SYSTEMS

Telemetry and the Future of Race Car Performance Analysis

The regulations for 1994 are an effort by FISA to reassert the importance of the driver over technology. Telemetry has become the byword for a system of instant data collection and monitoring of a race car's performance. The information gathered is used by the race teams in the never ending quest to increase overall performance. It enables the driver to compare his performance on different laps or against his teammate; it quantifies the effects of changes in the car set up; helps diagnose engine problems and helps optimise chassis and engine performance. Potentially the system has far reaching effects, but it's uses will be restricted next season as telemetry has become caught up in the arguments over traction control and active suspension.

Telemetry arrived in F1 in the late 1980's courtesy of the major engine manufacturers, in particular Honda, who led the way in the design and the development of the system. Tyrrell was first introduced to the system by Honda in 1991, but now uses a system by Pi Research, after its introduction to the team by it's engine supplier in 1992, Ilmor. The system currently used by the team can, in the words of Simon Barker, an engineer for the team, "be split into two, the engine and the chassis. We don't have an automatic gearbox, but most have a system for the gearbox as well. Basically, you have an system which gives you all the temperatures and pressures within the engine. For the chassis you have a system which gives you the ride heights of the car, hydraulic fluid pressure, suspension loadings or movements which can tell you, for instance, if the front wheels have come off the ground, or

The photograph shows the active suspension engineer download the information from the black box information centre on the car to the computer, this information is then fed to the mainframe computer where the engineers can view its performance on the screen.

The black box on the sidepod of the Lotus contains all the information gathered from the active suspension during practice, qualifying and the race, any journey the car makes is recorded.

The Lotus actuators on the F1 car seen here are different to the Williams arrangement, Lotus were indeed the first team to win a Grand Prix with an active car, Williams then became the second team to win using active, Senna and Piquet being the respective drivers.

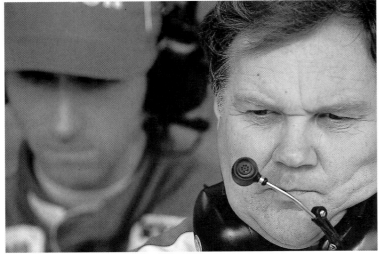

when the back wheels are overloaded or underloaded."

"The system can transmit and log information in two different ways. Information from the car can be sent back to the pits in "real time" as the car is running. Twenty channels are available to transmit information in this way. Another fifty channels are available to gather and store data on a logger, which is then downloaded onto a portable computer once the car is back in the pits. All of the information is collected by sensors and relayed to a Electronic Control Unit (E.C.U), which processes the information before it's stored in the logger. If the information is sent back in "real time" it is transmitted back directly from the E.C.U.", says Barker.

The system used by Tyrrell only transmits from the car to the pits. The system used by Williams-Renault, for example, is on a different level of sophistication. Williams-Renault can transmit from the pits to the car. It is possible with such a system to, for example, change the fuel mixture during the race, without the driver knowing. Pits to car is banned for 1994.

The Pi Research system, as used by Tyrrell, allows downloading in a mere 20 seconds and

the information can then be made available in a variety of formats for analysis. Histograms, for example, can show the proportion of time spent in each RPM band for a lap or complete session. Telltale Report's show the maximum and minimum values for each parameter for each lap, allowing a quick check that nothing is out of range. Graphs for either one lap or an entire race can be overlaid to allow instant comparisons.

Access to this information has allowed drivers to analyse their laps in great detail. Barker explains, "It is used as tool by the drivers. After every session the driver get's a print out and we go through it with him. You can then overlay both drivers' speeds and times on the track and say "He's quicker than you here, but slower there", so you can tell the drivers "If you can do that here, and what he is doing there, you'll both be quicker".

The logged information is vital when fine tuning the car to a particular circiut, especially if the team has active suspension and traction control. The system has a lateral accelerometer built into the control box and can automatically make and draw a map of the circuit from a typical lap of logged data. The team can adjust the map until they are satisfied with it and then apply this map to all the data from that circuit, allowing accurate comparisons of runs to be done on a corner by corner and straight by straight basis. "When applying the information to an active system", says Barker "teams spend a lot of time analysing every movement in the suspension system to find out if it is moving in the right place, because it could be moving either too early or too late. So by inspecting the information we can judge whether the movement should be ten meters earlier or later. With traction control you can try to tune it so that when the driver is half way into the corner he can floor it and keep his foot in."

Where could telemetry ultimately go? According to Barker, telemetry in conjunction with traction control, ABS braking, active suspension and four wheel steering could result in a system where all the driver would have to do is to keep the right line around the track. "With such a system you could measure the slip angle of the tyres and G forces, so the driver knows that when he goes into a corner he has got to turn three degrees. That's the corner, and the car will do the rest". FISA has steered F1 away from such a course by banning traction control and active suspension for 1994. Telemetry will primarily revert to performing its original function, that of gathering data so as to monitor the performance of the engine. For those teams which pay for engine supply, the cost of an engine is a significant proportion of the seaon's budget. As Barker says, "Millions of pounds have been saved, because the telemetry system will tell you immediately if the engine has a problem. We can inform the driver and save the engine".

Patrick Head and Damon Hill, the two men who between them developed and tested the semi-automatic gearbox at Williams Grand Prix Engineering.

The Williams steering wheel which shows the gearchange mechanism, the driver pulls the plate on one side for an upchange and the other side for a downchange through the gearbox.

The Ligier Renault steering wheel showing a similar arrangement to the Williams semi-automatic gearchange.

The telemetry system which exists behind each and every pit garage resembles a Tyrrel-Yamaha engineers keep a watchful eye on Andrea De Cesaris during the Portuguese Grand Prix.

MICHELE ALBORETO	JEAN ALESI	PHILIPPE ALLIOT	MICHAEL ANDRETTI

(ITA), 23/12/1956	*(FRA) 11/6/1964*	*(FRA), 27/7/1954*	*(USA), 5/10/62*

Another of G.P.'s elder generation and a driver with a wealth of experience. Alboreto's glory days were with Ferrari from 1984 to 1988, after which he left upset by the treatment he was receiving. The highpoint of this period was when he was runner-up to Prost in the World Championship. Recent years have seen him battle to develop a series of chassis-engine combinations, the least memorable of which was the Footwork-Porsche. Despite this his speed and commitment are undiminished. Following a fine season in 1992 when he outpaced his teammate Suzuki he was chosen to spearhead the all new Lola-Ferrari team. The chassis-engine combination proved difficult from the start, but to his credit Alboreto has persisted. He deserves better before finishing his F1 career.

Alesi's arrival in F1 was like a breath of fresh air. Undaunted by the reputations of many of the more experienced GP drivers, his performances for Tyrrell were audacious. Typical of this fearlessness was an incident at a race in the U.S. in 1990 when on being passed by Senna for the lead, he passed Senna straight away on the next corner. Currently in his third season with Ferrari, his commitment to a team rent by politics is commendable. However, it is lamentable that he has not had machinery worthy of his talent. Few who witnessed the spectacle will forget the rapturous response of the tifosi to Alesi's performance at Monza this year.

Alliot has followed a similar career path to that of Derek Warwick in that at the end of the 1990 season he stepped down from F1 to re-establish his credentials with the Peugeot World Sports Car Team. His outright speed has never been in question, though some have critised the number of off-circuit excursions. 1993 saw the return of Alliot to F1 with the French Larrousse equipe and he scored the team's first points of the season at San Marino with an excellent 5th place. Perhaps this is evidence that he feels comfortable with the team and it is to be hoped that in such an enviroment he will match his undoubted speed with consistency.

Andretti entered F1 following a highly successful career in IndyCar racing. He has a reputation for outright speed and daring overtaking maneouvres. Leaving the American series for F1 without relevant European track experience was a big risk. His season started in the worst possible way with a series of spectacular accidents and no sooner had he grasped standing starts than he was dogged by technical problems. To his credit he persisted and Monza saw him take a podium finish. Shortly thereafter he announced that he would be returning to the U.S., which is a great loss to F1.

PALMARES

1980 - F3 European Champion
1982 - F1 Tyrrell-Ford. F2 Minardi.
1984 - F1 Ferrari, 4th.
1985 - F1 Ferrari, runner-up in the World Championship.
1986 - F1 Ferrari, 8th.
1987 - F1 Ferrari, 7th.
1988 - F1 Ferrari, 5th.
1991 - F1 Footwork-Porsche/Ford.
1992 - F1 Footwork-Mugen, 10th.
1993 - F1 BMS Scuderia Italia-Ferrari.

PALMARES

1987 - French F3 Championship/Oreca, Champion.
1989 - F3000/Eddie Jordan, European Champion. F1 Tyrrell-Ford, 8 G.P.s, 9th.
1990 - F1 Tyrrell-Ford, 9th.
1991 - F1 Ferrari, 7th.
1992 - F1 Ferrari, 7th.
1993 - F1 Ferrari.

PALMARES

1983 - F2 European Championship. Le Mans, 3rd.
1984 - F1 RAM-Hart.
1986 - F1 Ligier-Renault, 18th. F3000 EC/March.
1989 - F1 Larrousse-Lola-Ford, 16th.
1990 - F1 Ligier-Ford.
1991 - WSPC/Peugeot.
1992 - WSPC/Peugeot, World Championship runner-up.
1993 - F1 Larrousse-Lamborghini.

PALMARES

1982 - Formula Super Vee, Champion.
1983 - Formula Mondial, Champion.
1986 - CART/Kraco, runner-up.
1987 - CART/Kraco, runner-up.
1989 - CART/Newman-Haas, 3rd.
1990 - CART/Newman-Haas, runner-up.
1991 - CART/Newman-Haas, Champion.
1992 - CART/Newman-Haas, runner-up.
1993 - F1 Marlboro-McLaren-Ford.

MARCO APICELLA

(ITA), 7/10/1965

Apicella has been waiting in the wings of F3000 ready to breakthrough to F1. Considered by most in F3000 to be a fast and accomplished driver, for many years Apicella was the "nearly man" of that series. He was a consistent front-runner, but victory eluded him until he transfered to the Japanese series in 1992. His GP debut with Sasol-Jordan at Monza proved inconclusive. At the first corner both team cars were eliminated by an accident.

LUCA BADOER

(ITA), 25/1/1971

Badoer rose to prominence when in his first year in the formula he won the F3000 European Championship in 1992. It was a convincing win despite his having a car advantage in his Crypton Reynard. He came to F1 with a reputation for being fast and for having natural ability. He has had a demanding first season, often battling with his vastly more experienced teammate Alboreto for the last qualifying position on the grid in the ungainly Lola Ferrari.

FEDERICO BARBAZZA

(ITA), 2/4/1963

Barbazza has not taken the conventional route to F1. When unable to find a F3000 drive he abandoned Europe for the U.S.A.. He became ARS champion in his first season and finished an impressive 3rd at Indianapolis on his first visit to the speed way. He made the breakthrough to F1 in 1991 with the uncompetitive AGS, but never managed to qualify. To finish in the top six on two occasions with Minardi in the first half of the 1993 season was an excellent achievement. Sadly, he was replaced by Martini at the British GP.

RUBENS BARRICHELLO

(BRA), 23/5/1972

Barrichello is considered Brazil's brightest hope for the future. He waltzed through the junior categories, either a champion or frontrunner in each formulae contested. With abundant backing from his home country Barrichello started the year in the best possible way. In the changeable weather conditions that prevailed at the European GP at Donnington he gave a breathtaking display of car control that left many of the more experienced competitors embarrassed. Over the year he has been partnered by four different drivers, none of whom could equal him. He shines out from this season's F1 newcomers.

PALMARES

1986 - F3 Italian Championship, runner-up.
1987 - F3000 International Championship.
1989 - F3000 International Championship, 4th.
1991 - F3000 International Championship, 5th.
1992 - F3000 Japanese Championship.
1993 - F3000 Japanese Championship. F1 debut Sasol-Jordan.

PALMARES

1987 - 100ccm-Kart, Italian Champion.
1988 - Kart, Super-100ccm and international classes, Italian Champion.
1990 - Italian F3 Championship/MDR.
1991 - Italian F3 Championship/Supercars, 4th.
1992 - F 3000/Crypton, European Champion.
1993 - F1 BMS Scuderia Italia Ferrari.

PALMARES

1986 - American Racing Series, Champion.
1987 - Indianapolis 500, 3rd. CART Rookie of the Year.
1991 - F1 AGS.
1993 - F1 debut Minardi.

PALMARES

1981-1988 - Karting, 5 times Brazilian Champion.
1990 - Opel Lotus Euroseries, Champion.
1991 - British F3 Champion.
1992 - F3000/Barone Rampante, 3rd.
1993 - F1 Jordan Hart.

GERHARD BERGER	MARK BLUNDELL	THIERRY BOUTSEN	MARTIN BRUNDLE

(A), 27/8/1959	(GB), 8/4/1966	(BEL), 13/7/1957	(GB), 1/6/1959

Despite having driven for all the top teams, bar Williams, Berger has never been a serious candidate for the World Championship. Following his three years at McLaren and and his partnership there with Senna, he returned to Ferrari a more rounded driver. Whilst at McLaren he was often as quick as his teammate, but seemed to suffer more than his share of bad luck. At Ferrari his teammate Alesi poses as great a challenge as Senna did, but Berger has risen to that challenge. His qualifying and racing performances demonstrate that he is still hungry for success and his exciting driving style assures him of a popular following.

Blundell prepared for his entry into F1 racing with a period as test driver with both Williams and McLaren. Working with the two top teams was invaluable experience. His performances in the uncompetitive Braham Yamaha alongside his vastly experienced Brundle were impressive and marked him as a driver to watch. Victory at the Peugeot World Sports Car Team at Le Mans brought him to the attention of the French. His performances with Brundle at Ligier have at long last changed the fortunes of the ambitious French team.

Boutsen is amongst the most experienced of GP drivers. It was still a surprise, however, after his departure from Ligier at the end of 1992 to see him back in F1 this year when he took over he Jordan seat vacated by Capelli. This season has proved a disappointment. He could not match the pace of his teammate Barrichello and retired gracefully after the Belgian GP, which marked his tenth year in F1.

Brundle was the only driver to have challenged Senna in F3 and both came to F1 in the same year. Since then their career paths have diverged. After four frustrating years with Tyrrell and Zakspeed Brundle left F1 to join the Jaguar sports car team and became World Champion in 1988. Victory at Le Mans in 1990 heralded his return to GP racing with Brabham. His big break came when he signed for Benetton in 1992 and after a difficult start by mid season his performances were shadowing those of teammate Schumacher. After the disappointment of not landing a McLaren or Williams drive for 1993 he signed for Ligier. He has helped revitalise the well-funded French team with a number of excellent podium finishes.

PALMARES

1984 - F3 European Championship, 3rd. F3 G.P. Monaco, runner-up. F1 ATS-BMW, from G.P. Austria onwards.
1985 - F1 Arrows-BMW, 17th.
1986 - F1 Benetton-BMW, 7th. 1st GP victory, Mexico.
1987 - F1 Ferrari, 5th.
1988 - F1 Ferrari, 3rd.
1990 - F1 Marlboro-McLaren-Honda, 3rd.
1993 - F1 Ferrari.

PALMARES

1986 - EFDA FF 2000, Champion.
1988 - F3000 EC/Lola, 6th.
1989 - F3000 EC/Lola. WSPC/Nissan.
1990 - WSPC/Nissan. F1 Williams-Renault Test Driver.
1991 - F1 Brabham-Yamaha, 18th.
1992 - F1 Marlboro McLaren-Honda Test Driver. WSPC/Peugeot, Le Mans Winner.
1993 - F1 Ligier-Renault.

PALMARES

1980 - F3 EC, 2nd. Belgian F3 Champion.
1981 - F2 European Championship, 2nd.
1983 - F1 Arrows-Ford.
1987 - F1 Benetton-Ford, 8th.
1989 - F1 Williams-Renault, 5th. 1st GP victory in Canada.
1990 - F1 Williams-Renault, 6th.
1991 - F1 Ligier-Lamborghini.
1992 - F1 Ligier-Renault, 14th.
1993 - F1 Jordan-Hart.

PALMARES

1983 - British F3 Championship, runner-up behind Senna.
1984 - F1 Tyrrell-Ford.
1987 - F1 Zakspeed, 18th.
1988 - WSPC with Jaguar, World Champion.
1989 - F1 Brabham-Judd, 16th.
1990 - WSPC with Jaguar, Le Mans winner.
1991 - F1 Brabham-Yamaha, 15th.
1992 - F1 Benetton-Ford, 6th.
1993 - F1 Ligier-Renault.

IVAN CAPELLI

(ITA), 24/5/1963

There was a period in Capelli's career when he was a much sought after driver. Excellent performances for March between 1988 and 1990 saw him challenge on occasions for outright victory. In retrospect the collapse of March in 1991 marked the collapse of Capelli's career. The dream move to Ferrari was not the success he would have hoped for. The bad luck he suffered at Ferrari followed him to Sasol-Jordan and Brazil was his last drive for the team.

ERICK COMAS

(FRA), 28/9/1963.

Comas is one of the great hopes of French racing. He had a meteoric rise in the junior formula, winning every championship he contested. Life in F1 has not been so straightforward. His two years with Ligier proved to be a frustrating experience as two different chassis-engine combinations were being developed. Further, Comas was not helped by a virtually non-existent relationship with his vastly more experienced teammate, Boutsen. There is little question that Comas possesses the talent to suceed.

ANDREA DE CESARIS

(ITA), 31/5/1959

In his 13th full season in F1, de Cesaris has a wealth of experience with a wide variety of teams. Now approaching his 200th GP he is the most experienced driver never to have won a race. No longer the wild driver of his youth he is still highly competitive and worthy of a more competitive car. The steady progress made by the underfinanced Tyrrell-Yamaha team can in part be attributed to his valuable technical input.

CHRISTIAN FITTIPALDI

(BRA), 18/1/1971

Fittipaldi's first season in F1 in 1992 showed that the young Brazilian had the speed and maturity to follow in his uncle Emerson's footsteps. Neither a reckless nor a careless driver it is unfortunate that he has suffered two big accidents so early on in his F1 career. He took some time to recover from the accident at Magny-Cours, but he bounced back scoring Championship points in Japan. With a Ford engined car for 1993 he immediatley showed his mettle by scoring points at the season opener in South Africa. It is to be hoped that the spectacular accident on the last lap at Monza with teammate Martini, in which his car almost crossed the chequered flag mid air, has not dented his confidence.

PALMARES

1976 - Junior Kart World Champion.
1981 - F1 McLaren-Ford.
1983 - F1 Alfa Romeo, 8th in the World Championship.
1984 - F1 Ligier-Renault.
1986 - F1 Minardi-Motori Moderni.
1987 - F1 Brabham-BMW.
1988 - F1 Rial-Ford.
1989 - F1 Dallara-Ford.
1991 - F1 Jordan-Ford, 9th in the World Championship.
1992 - F1 Tyrrell-Ilmor, 9th in the World Championship.
1993 - F1 Tyrrell-Yamaha.

PALMARES

1984 - French Renault 5 Cup. Winer "Volant Elf-Winfield".
1986 - French Formula Renault Champion.
1988 - French F3 Champion. F3 G.P. Monaco, runner-up.
1990 - F3000 European Champion.
1991 - F1 Ligier-Lamborghini.
1992 - F1 Ligier-Renault, 11th.
1993 - F1 Larrousse-Lamborghini.

PALMARES

198 - F3 European Championship, Champion.
1985 - F1 Tyrrell Renault.
1987 - F1 March.
1992 - F1 Ferrari.
1993 - F1 Sasol-Jordan. 2 GPs.

PALMARES

1990 - F3 British Championship, 4th. F3 South American Champion.
1991 - F3000 EC/Pacific, European Champion.
1992 - F1 Minardi-Lamborghini, 17th.
1993 - F1 Minardi-Ford.

JEAN MARC GOUNON	MIKA HAKKINEN	JOHNNY HERBERT	DAMON HILL

JEAN MARC GOUNON

(FRA), 1/1/1963

MIKA HAKKINEN

(SF), 28/9/1968

JOHNNY HERBERT

(GB), 27/6/1964

DAMON HILL

(GB), 17/09/1960

Following three years in F3000 Jean-Marc Gounon has earned himself a reputation as a quick and reliable performer. Earlier this season his hopes of a GP drive were dashed when March, with whom he had hoped to drive, withdrew from the Championship. Gounon did little competitive driving this season and did not test with Minardi, so his disappointing performance at Suzuka should not have come as a surprise.

Hakkinen, a natural talent, missed the greater part of the 1993 season until the sudden departure of Andretti. While at Lotus he was well matched with Herbert. By joining McLaren at the end of 1992 he risked all in the hope that Senna would take a sabbatical. Senna's decision to race this season left Hakkinen high and dry. He is keen to demonstrate his talent and now faces the ultimate comparison as teammate to Senna.

Until a horrific accident at Brands Hatch in 1988 in F3000, Herbert had seemed set for an early move to F1. A premature comeback straight into F1 with Benetton proved ill-advised, Herbert having not fully recovered from his injuries. It was not until 1991 that the career of the talented Herbert got back on course, when he was re-united at Lotus with Peter Collins, his team manager and admirer from the Benetton days. Both parties have shown loyalty to each other and Lotus could not have made a better and more popular choice to head their revival.

There can be few drivers with so little F1 experience who have landed a plum GP drive. Damon's performances in the uncompetitive Brabham were hard to gauge in 1992 . However, thousands of miles testing for Williams convinced the team management that Damon could fill the void left by the departing Mansell. After an embarrassing debut with the team in South Africa, his performances have been a revelation. Quick in qualifing, and a shrewd tactician, he has consistently challenged his vastly more experienced teammate, and proved that he can win races on merit, and is worthy of a seat with currently the best team in GP racing.

PALMARES

1986 Formula Renault, runner-up.
1987 Formula Renault, runner-up.
1989 French Formula 3, Champion.
1990 European F3000, 9th.
1991 European F3000, 6th.
1992 European F3000, 6th.
1993 GP debut, Minardi Ford.

PALMARES

1988 - Opel Lotus Euroseries, Champion.
1990 - F3 British Championship, Champion.
1991 - F1 Lotus-Judd, 15th.
1992 - F1 Lotus-Judd, 8th.
1993 - F1 Marlboro-McLaren-Ford.

PALMARES

1985 - British Formula Ford 1600, Winner Formula Ford Festival, Brands Hatch.
1987 - British F3 Championship, Champion.
1988 - F3000/Eddie Jordan.
1989 - F1 Benetton-Ford/Tyrrell-Ford, 14th.
1990 - F3000 at Japan. F1 Lotus-Lamborghini.
1991 - F1 Lotus-Judd.
1992 - F1 Lotus-Ford, 14th.
1993 - F1 Lotus-Ford.

PALMARES

1988 - British F3 Championship, 3rd overall. Macao GP, F3, 2nd.
1989 - European F3000
1990 - European F3000, 13th overall.
1991 - European F3000, 7th overall.
1992 - F1 Brabham-Judd.
1993 - F1 Williams-Renault, 1st F1 victory, Hungarian GP.

EDDIE IRVINE

(N.I.), 10/11/1965

When Irvine made his GP debut at his adopted home track of Susuka he was racing against many of his old Formula Ford adversaries for the first time since 1985. His career in recent years has taken a different turn to those of his contemporaries. After two disappointing years in European F3000, he was invited to drive for the Cerumo Team in Japanese F3000, where he quickly established himself. He has proved to be a consistent front runner in a highly competitive series. Meanwhile, he has not been forgotten in Europe. At Le Mans this year he was consistently the fastest driver. Although firmly esconsed in Japan, he is keen to compete with old rivals.

┌─ PALMARES ─┐

1987 - Victory in two senior Formula Ford Championships and Formula Ford Festival.
1988 - F3 British Championship, runner-up.
1989 - European F3000.
1990 - European F3000, third. Macao GP, third.
1991 -
1993 Japanese F3000. Group C Sports Cars for SARD and Toyota.
GP debut, Sasol Jordan.

UKYO KATAYAMA

(JAP), 26/5/63

Katayama arrived in F1 in 1992 as the current Japanese F3000 Champion and with substantial backing from his native country. Some observed that the step to F1 was a bigger one than Katayama had anticipated, but during his debut year there were moments when he showed both courage and speed. This season Katayama has gained valuable F1 experience despite having to contend with the problems posed to a driver by chassis and engine development.

┌─ PALMARES ─┐

1988 - Japanese F3000, 11th.
1990 - Japanese F3000, 5th.
1991 - Japanese F3000, Champion.
1992 - F1 Venturi-Larrousse-Lamborghini.
1993 - F1 Tyrrell-Yamaha.

PEDRO LAMY

(PORT), 20/3/1972

Lamy is one of the most talented drivers to emerge from Portugal in recent years and may prove to be the country's first regular GP driver in more than a generation. He is quick and has ample domestic support. Victory in the GM Lotus Euroseries in 1991 and the German F3 Championship the following year have marked him a man to watch. Having made the move to F3000 he has been criticised for his erratic driving style, however, his GP debut with Lotus at Monza showed a mature approach.
Only mechanical failure stopped him from finishing in the top ten.

┌─ PALMARES ─┐

1989 - National Formula Ford Championship, Champion.
1991 - GM Lotus Euroseries, Champion.
1992 - F3 German Championship, Champion.
1993 - F3000 International Championship. F1 debut with Team Lotus.

JIRKI JARVI LEHTO

(SF) 31/1/1966

Lehto was heralded as a bright new star when he arrived in F1. He was almost unbeatable in FF2000 and F3, racing with the best teams. Lehto was not as lucky with his drives during his formative years in F1. As such it has been hard to make a meaningful comparison between his F1 performances. Undoubtedly brave and with abundant natural talent, he has comfortably matched the performances of his highly rated teammate during the 1993 season driving for the impressive new Sauber team.

┌─ PALMARES ─┐

1987 - FF 2000, British Championship, Champion. EFDA Euroseries, Champion. Formel Ford Weltcup, Champion.
1988 - F3, British Championship, Champion. F3 GP Macao, 1st.
1989 - F3000 EC/Pacific, 13th. F1 Onyx-Ford, 2 GP starts.
1990 - F1 Onyx-Monteverdi-Ford, 5 GPs starts.
1991 - F1 Scuderia Italia Dallara-Judd, 12th.
1992 - F1 Scuderia Italia, Dallara-Ferrari.
1993 - F1 Sauber.

PIERLUIGI MARTINI

(ITA), 23/4/1961

Martini was much maligned when he entered F1 in 1985 with Minardi. A period in F3000 boosted his confidence before he re-entered the GP arena in 1988, again with Minardi. He is now widely respected in GP circles, his speed and commitment never in doubt and, in particular, he is highly regarded by Giancarlo Minardi. He rejoined Minardi at the British GP replacing Fabrizio Barbazza and his performance in the underfunded Minardi at Hungary was a revelation, especially when compared with the better financed high-technology teams.

FABRIZIO E. NASPETTI

(ITA) 24/2/1968

Naspetti's success in the Italian F3 Championship was followed by two inconclusive years in F3000 until a move to Forti Corse revitalised his career. He finished 3rd with the team in 1991 and in 1992 left mid season when lying 2nd to pursue his F1 ambitions. He made his F1 debut with the struggling March team and his performances alongside his highly-rated teammate Wendlinger were impressive.

RICCARDO PATRESE

(ITA), 17/4/1954

Hockenheim marked Riccardo Patrese's 250th GP, which means that he has raced more GPs than any other driver in history. In a long and illustrious career, Patrese has experienced the highs and lows of F1 racing culminating in runner-up in the World Championship to teammate Nigel Mansell in 1992. A much-liked figure in this most competitive of sports, his move to Benetton this season has proved difficult, but the support and experience he brings to any team is to be valued.

ALAIN PROST

(FRA), 24/02/1955

Before the start of the season some observers questioned Prost's speed and commitment following his sabbatical year. The doubters should have realised that any driver of Prost's calibre should not be discounted before the first race. His fourth World Championship and first with Renault will no doubt help both parties to forget the injustice of losing the Championship in 1983. Throughout the season Prost, now 38, demonstrated his legendary speed and technical ability. Despite having a car advantage victory did not always come easily, especially given the competitiveness of his ambitious teammate.

┌─ PALMARES ─┐

1983 - F3 European Champion (Ralt-Alfa-Romeo).
1985 - F1 Minardi-Ford/-Turbo.
1986 - F3000.
1990 - F1 Minardi-Ford.
1991-F1 Minardi-Ferrari, 11th.
1992 - Dallara-Ferrari, 14th.
1993 - Minardi-Ford.

┌─ PALMARES ─┐

1988 - F3 Italian Championship, Champion.
1991 - F3000 International Championship, 3rd.
1992 - F3000 International Championship. F1 debut with March.
1993 - F3000 Japanese Championship. F1 Sasol-Jordan.

┌─ PALMARES ─┐

1974 - Kart World Champion.
1976 - F3, Italian and European Champion.
1977 - F1 Shadow.
1982 - F1 Brabham-Ford/BMW, 1st GP victory at Monaco.
1983 - F1 Brabham-BMW, 9th in the World Championship.
1989 - F1 Williams-Renault, 3rd in the World Championship.
1990 - F1 Williams-Renault, 7th in the World Championship.
1991 - F1 Williams-Renault, 3rd in the World Championship.
1992 - F1 Williams-Renault, runner-up in the World Championship.
1993 - F1 Benetton-Ford.

┌─ PALMARES ─┐

1978 - French F3, Champion.
1979 - European F3, Champion.
1983 - F1 Renault, runner-up in World Championship.
1984 - F1 McLaren-Tag, runner-up World Championship.
1985 - F1 McLaren-Tag, World Champion.
1986 - F1 McLaren-Tag, World Champion.
1988 - F1 McLaren-Honda, runner-up World Championship.
1989 - F1 McLaren-Honda, World Champion.
1990 - F1 Ferrari, runner-up World Championship.
1993 - F1 Williams-Renault, World Champion.

MICHAEL SCHUMACHER	AYRTON SENNA	AGURI SUZUKI	TOSHIO SUZUKI

(D) 3/1/1969	*(BRA), 21/3/1960*	*(JAP), 8/9/1960*	*(JAP), 10/3/1955*

When talking about Schumacher it is hard not to gush about his natural talent and ability. Since his debut at Spa expectations have been high and he has yet to disappoint. Experience has brought maturity to his driving and this season his qualifying performances have been consistently breathtaking and his race performances, which are equally impressive, have been memorable for his audacious overtaking manouvres.

The Brazilian triple world champion started the season on a race by race basis, only confirming his participation for the full season after protracted negotiations with McLaren and Ford over the supply of the latest HB V8's to the team. His challenge to the all powerful Williams-Renault in the early part of the season saw Senna at his brilliant best. The chassis was not truly competitive, not in the sense that one has come to expect from McLaren, but this only made the Brazilian's resolution to take the battle to his great rival Prost even greater.

The highlight of Suzuki's career came in front of his home crowd at the Japanese GP in 1990 when he finished an excellent third position. It was a highly accomplished performance and many expected his career to take off, however, that has yet to happen. The following season proved very disappointing. 1993 saw glimpses of Suzuki's form of three years ago. He has matched teammate Warwick for pace and has run comfortably in the top ten in the latter half of the season with the rejuvenated Footwork chassis.

At the age of 38, Toshio Suzuki achieved a long held ambition when he made his GP debut at Suzuka. He first came to prominence in the early '80s when competing in F3 in Europe. After two years he returned to Japan to forge a career as a versatile journeyman. His best result came at Daytona in 1991. His previous GP experience is that of engine testing for Williams-Honda in 1987 at Suzuka. Unfortunately, lack of testing with Larrousse meant that he was unable to capitalise on his knowledge of the circuit at his GP debut.

PALMARES

1987 - Kart-European Champion, German Champion.
1989 - F3 German Championship, 3rd.
1990 - WSPC Sauber-Mercedes, 1 victory, 5th. German F3 Champion. Winner F3 G.P. Fuji.
1991 - WSPC Sauber-Mercedes. F1 Jordan-Ford/Benetton-Ford.
1992 - F1 Benetton-Ford, 1st GP victory Spa.
1993 - F1 Benetton-Ford.

PALMARES

1983 - British F3, Champion.
1984 - F1 Toleman-Hart, 9th.
1985 - F1 Lotus-Renault, 1st GP victory.
1988 - F1 McLaren-Honda, World Champion.
1989 - F1 McLaren-Honda, runner up.
1990 - F1 McLaren-Honda, World Champion.
1991 _ F1 McLaren-Honda, World Champion.
1993 _ F1 McLaren-Ford.

PALMARES

1983 - Japanese F3, runner-up.
1987 - Japanese F3000, runner-up.
1988 - Japanese F3000, Champion.
1989 - F1 Zakspeed.
1990 - F1 Larrousse-Lola-Lamborghini, 10th.
1991 - F1 Larrousse-Lola-Ford.
1992 - F1 Footwork-Mugen.
1993 - F1 Footwork-Mugen.

PALMARES

1979 Japanese F3, Champion.
1980 British and European F3.
1982 Japanese F2.
1987 Japanese F3000.
1991 Daytona 24 Hours, NISMO, winner.
1993 24 Hour Le Mans, 4th; GP debut, Larrousse Lamborghini.

DEREK WARWICK

(GB), 27/8/1954

Warwick has twice abandoned F1 to take topline sports car drives with Jaguar and Peugeot. He grabbed at the chance when given the opportunity to return. Over the years a number of uncompetitive drives have not allowed him to show his true worth. Warwick never gives less than his best and is one of the most likeable and approachable of drivers in the F1 paddock. His technical ability have helped develop the FA14 into a potentially consistent points scorer in the latter half of the 1993 season.

KARL WENDLINGER

(AUT) 20/12/1968

Wendlingers path to GP racing was helped by felow Austrian Gerhard Berger. A contemporary and teammate of Michael Schumacher in the Mercedes Sports Car Team, he firmly believes that given the equipment he can produce the same results as the German. Given the machinery at his disposal at underfunded March he impressed many in 1992 with his qualifying and race performances. In 1993 Wendlinger was back with Sauber, who had formed the backbone of the Mercedes Sports Car Team. Excellent qualifying performances during the early part of the season and point scoring finishes have proved that Wendlinger has made consistent progress during the year.

ALESSANDRO ZANARDI

(ITA), 23/10/1966

The unexpected driver vacancy that arose at Team Lotus following Mika Hakkinen's departure was filled by another rising star, Zanardi, an aggressive racer and accomplished test driver. His career credentials are excellent, with wins in every championship competed in outside F1. In 1991 he only narrowly failed to win the F3000 Championship in his first year. Two fine races in a Jordan at the end of that year confirmed him as being worthy of an F1 drive. Zanardi's season in 1993 was interrupted by an enormous accident in qualifying at Spa. It remains to be seen how quickly he can recover from this.

PALMARES

1987 - FF1600, Austrian Champion. German FF1600 Championship, 6th.
1988 - F3, Austrian Champion. German F3 Championship, 10th.
1989 - German F3 Championship, Champion.
1990 - WSPC/Sauber-Mercedes, 5th. F3000 EC/Marko. German Touring Car Championship/Mercedes.
1991 - Sportwagen-WM/Sauber-Mercedes. F3000 EC/Marko.
F1 Leyton House-Ilmor, 2 GPs
1992 - F1 March-Ilmor, 12th.
1993 - F1 Sauber.

PALMARES

1978 - British F3 Championship, runner up.
1981 - Toleman-Hart, debut season.
1984 - F1 Renault, 7th.
1986 - WSPC, Jaguar, runner up.
1988 - F1 Arrows-Megatron, 7th.
1990 - F1 Lotus-Lamborghini, 14th.
1991 - WSPC, Jaguar, runner up.
1992 - WSPC, Peugeot, World Champion.
1993 - F1 Footwork-Mugen.

PALMARES

1986 - Italian Kart Champion
1990 - Italian F3 Championship, runner-up. Winner FIA F3 European Cup, Le Mans.
1991 - F3000 EC/Barone Rampante, runner-up.
1992 - F1 Minardi-Lamborghini. F1 Benetton test driver.
1993 - F1 Lotus-Ford.

HUNGARORING

Dopo il loro successo a Indy,
pochi avrebbero creduto che i
telai della Lola si sarebbero
rivelati così poco competitivi.
Michele Alboreto, che vi ha speso
mille e mille volte il meglio di sé,
ne ha ricavato solo posizioni di
nessun conto in graduatoria e una
serie di mancati arrivi.

*Following their Indycar success
few would have believed at the
start of the season that the Lola
chassis could have proved SO
uncompetative. Michele
Alboreto time and time again
gave his all only to be rewarded
with lowly grid positions and a
series of non finishes.*

HUNGARORING

Le migliaia di tifosi che passarono
la frontiera dell'Austria solo per
seguire Berger, sono stati
ricompensati dal connazionale
con una prestazione vittoriosa.
Gerhard ha diviso l'accoglienza
offerta a Schumacher sul podio di
Hockenheim, in Ungheria: le
bandiere austriache sventolavano
ovunque.
(Nella pagina precedente)

*The thousands of fans who
crossed the border from Austria
to watch Berger, were rewarded
with a typically inspired
performance from their fellow
countryman. Gerhard enjoyed
the reception given to
Schumacher at Hockenheim at
the podium in Hungary,
Austrian flags were everywhere.*
(Preceding page)

HUNGARORING

Damon Hill ha assaporato gli alti
e bassi delle corse del Gran
Premio in sole due settimane; la
prima vittoria al Gran Premio,
abbondantemente meritata, non è
arrivata in un momento troppo
precoce ed è stata bene accolta
da tutti; il pubblico del paddock si
è esaltato per Damon quando è
riapparso dopo le interviste
rilasciate al traguardo della corsa.
Un vincitore davvero popolare:
congratulazioni Damon!

*Damon Hill tasted the highs
and lows of Grand Prix racing
within a two week period, his
richly deserved first Grand Prix
victory came not a moment too
soon and was welcomed by all.
The paddock cheered Damon as
he returned from the post race
interviews, a truly popular
winner, congratulations Damon.*

HUNGARORING

Luca Badoer, in una ripresa spettacolare; mentre Schumacher lo sta superando, non è riuscito a rimaner in traiettoria e ha regalato così ai fotografi la possibilità di immortalare interessanti momenti del fine settimana.

Luca Badoer in spectacular fashion, while being lapped by Schumacher failed to negotiate the corner and provided the photographers with some interesting material from the weekend.

HUNGARORING

Il sempre popolare e spettacolare Alesi ancora una volta ha superato brillantemente l'esame durante le qualificazioni; sfortunatamente per la corsa non ha condiviso il successo del suo compagno di squadra Berger e ha concluso la gara contro la barriera della prima curva.

The ever popular and spectacular Alesi once again proved good viewing during qualifying, unfortunately for the race he did not sahre the success of team mate Berger and ended his race against the barrier at the first corner.

HUNGARORING

Il ritorno di Martini alla Minardi e la sua rinnovata intesa con Giancarlo si sono rivelati la combinazione vincente. Durante la sessione ungherese, la forza motrice degli Italiani, pur essendo contenuta, ha eclissato l'abilità di molte squadre tecnicamente più avanzate.

Martini's return to Minardi and his re acquaintance with Giancarlo proved a successful partnership. The diminutive Italians drive at the Hungaroring shamed many of the more technically advanced teams.

SPA-FRANCORCHAMPS

I giovani campioni del Gran Premio in pista a Spa Franchorchamps. Damon Hill e Michael Schumacher con le loro prestazioni di questa stagione hanno infiammato i circuiti della Formula Uno.
(Nella pagina accanto)

The Grand Prix young guns go for it at Spa-Franchorchamps, Damon Hill and Michael Schumacher have set the Formula One paddock alight with their performances this season.
(Opposite)

SPA-FRANCORCHAMPS

La McLaren di Senna doppia La
Source Hairpin avviandosi al
quarto piazzamento al traguardo.
Questo risultato è stato deludente
per Senna, dopo un fine
settimana difficile sia per lui sia
per il manager della squadra, Ron
Dennis.

*Senna's McLaren rounds La
Source hairpin on it's way to
fourth place, a dissapointment
for Senna after a frustrating
weekend for both him and team
owner Ron Dennis.*

SPA-FRANCORCHAMPS

L'approccio alle corse di Michele Alboreto, il cui motto è non arrendersi mai, si è rivelato ancora necessario per ottenere la massima prestazione dalla Lola-Ferrari a Spa Franchorchamps.

Michele Alboreto's never say die approach to racing was needed yet again to extract the utmost performance from the Lola Ferrari at Spa-Franchorchamps.

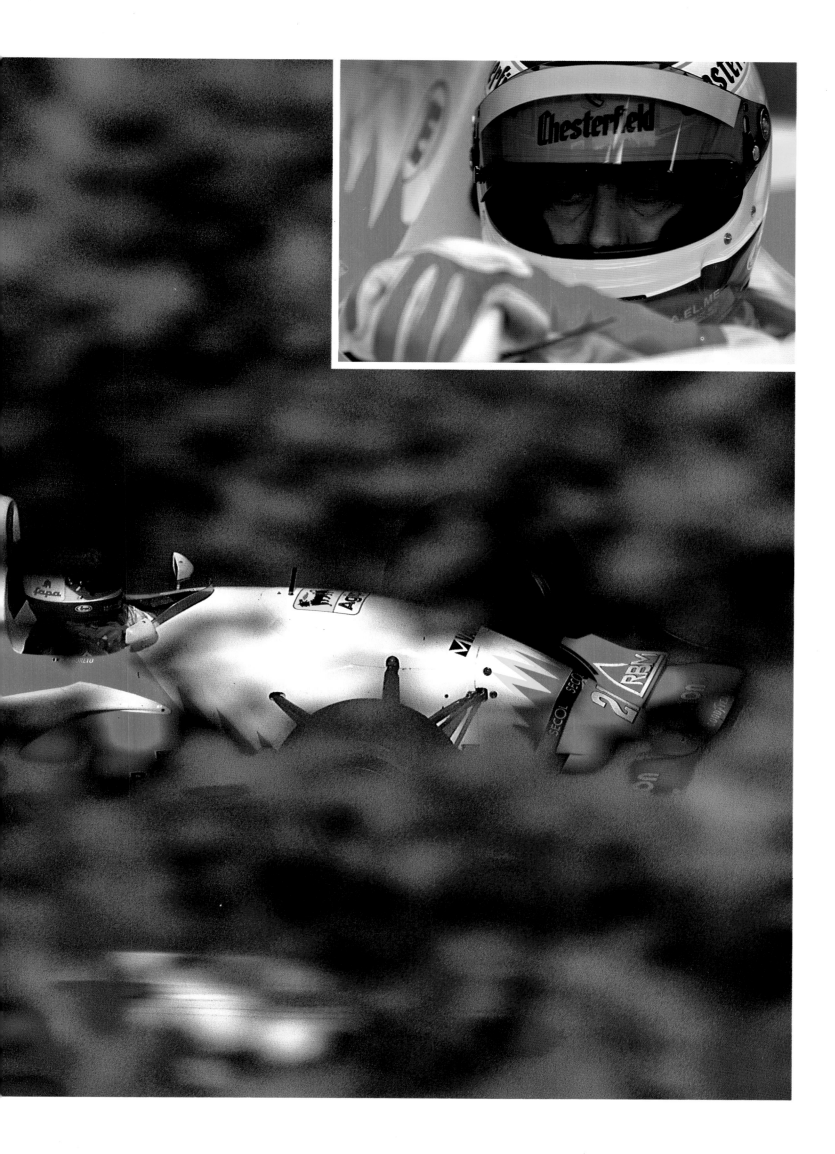

SPA-FRANCORCHAMPS

Alain Prost ha realizzato senza dubbio la migliore partenza della stagione a Spa. Un peggioramento della guidabilità, però, lo ha fatto concludere al terzo posto.

Alain Prost made what was undoubtedly his best start of the season at Spa only to suffer deteriorating handling which eventually resulted in third place after an encoouraging start.

SPA-FRANCORCHAMPS

La foresta delle Ardenne avvolge il circuito del Gran Premio con uno scenario da considerarsi forse tra i più spettacolari e sorprendenti del campionato. Qui Damon Hill infrange il placido silenzio sfrecciando con fragore verso la sua seconda vittoria.

The Ardenne Forest provides the Grand Prix circus with arguably the most spectacular and breathtaking backdrop in the Championship, here Damon Hill shatters the calm as he screeches through to his second victory.

Michael Schumacher festeggia dopo il magnifico recupero che lo ha portato dall'undicesima posizione alla seconda a fine gara: un'altra schiacciante conferma per il giovane tedesco.
(Foto piccola)

Michael Schumacher celebrates after his magnificient recovery drive through the field from eleventh at the first corner to second at the finish, yet another crushing performance from the young German.
(Small picture)

MONZA

A Monza Damon Hill ha dimostrato di essere indubbiamente un avversario da non sottovalutare. Damon ha condotto quella che, fino a questo punto, si può definire probabilmente la sua gara più aggressiva e tecnicamente equilibrata; dopo le schermaglie alla partenza con Senna, alla chicane Goodyear, ha lottato per risalire le posizioni fino a Prost, a pochi giri dall'arrivo. La sfortuna ha abbandonato Hill per accanirsi con Prost, il cui motore si è bloccato. A Damon è toccato l'emozionante trionfo di Monza, la sua terza vittoria successiva in un Gran Premio.
(Nella pagina seguente)

Damon Hill proved at Monza that he is most definitely a force to be reckoned with in Grand Prix racing. Damon drove probably his most aggressive and controlled race to date, after an altercation with Senna ate the Goodyear chicane at the start he fought his way up to Prost with only a handful of laps remaining. For a change Hills share of bad luck was meted out to Prost and his engine expired, leaving Damon with an emotional win at Monza, his third Grand Prix win in succession.
(Following page)

MONZA

Jean Alesi, il Villeneuve dei nostri giorni, col numero di gara 27. La sua rossa Ferrari ha sfrecciato con eleganza lungo il circuito di Monza, accompagnata dalle urla di sostegno della tifoseria. Jean, che ha spremuto dal motore V12 ogni cavallo di potenza, ha regalato alla folla intense emozioni, compiendo spettacolari sterzate. Per la Ferrari e la Pioneer, la squadra di casa e lo sponsor del Gran Premio d'Italia, è stata una giornata memorabile, così come per le migliaia di fedelissimi che hanno salutato Jean sulla linea di arrivo di Monza e sul podio.

Jean Alesi, the modern day Villeneuve, running No 27, his scarlet Ferrari danced its way around Monza, with the added volume of support from the Tifosi, Jean squeezed every ounce of horsepower from the V12 entertaining the crowd with every turn of the wheel. It was a memorable day for Ferrari & Pioneer, the team and Italian Grand Prix sponsor as well as the thousands of loyal fans who greeted Jean on the sacred Monza pit lane and podium.

MONZA

L'avvio del Gran Premio d'Italia è
stato uno tra i più emozionanti
degli ultimi tempi; il fumo denso
dei pneumatici è rimasto nell'aria
per almeno tre giri; solo quando
la cortina si è diradata il pubblico
ha potuto scoprire che si erano
ritirati tre piloti, Derek Warwick
e Aguri Suzuki, delle Footwork
Mugen Honda, e Marco Apicella
su Jordan alla sua prima
esperienza.

Anche la fine della gara è stata
carica di eventi: Christian
Fittipaldi è stato sbalzato sopra il
posteriore della vettura del suo
compagno di squadra Martini e si
è ribaltato a mezz'aria; in questa
immagine sta esaminando
nervosamente i resti della sua
Minardi.

L' epilogo delle qualificazioni finali
del sabato, per un'incomprensione
tra i due piloti Ferrari, Alesi e
Berger, si è tramutato quasi in un
disastro: Berger ha toccato il retro
del veicolo del suo compagno di
squadra e ha perso il controllo
dell'auto, arrestandosi contro la
barriera di pneumatici. La
fotografia mostra Gerhard mentre
viene tratto dai rottami ancora in
considerevole stato di shock dopo
l'impatto; tra i due piloti della
Ferrari tutto si è chiarito quando
Berger ha spiegato che stava
ancora percorrendo un giro di
qualificazione di cui non aveva
visto la bandiera a scacchi che ne
indicava la fine.

*The start of the Pioneer Italian
Grand Prix was the most
fraught seen in several races,
the tyre smoke hung in the air
for the following three laps,
when it cleared it revealed the
retirement of the two Footwork
Mugen Honda drivers, Derek
Warwick and Aguri Suzuki as
well as the one time Jordan
driver Marco Apicella.
The end of the race was also
full of incident when Christian
Fittipaldi vaulted over the rear
of his team-mate Martini and
somersaulted in mid air, here he
nervously examines the reamins
of his Minardi.
The end of final qualifying on
Saturday saw a
misunderstanding between the
Ferrari drivers Alesi and Berger
nearly end in disaster when
Berger touched the rear of his
team-mate's car and lost control
coming to rest by the tyre
barrier. The photograph shows
Gerhard being lifted from the
wreckage still in considerable
shock after the impact. All was
well between the two Ferrari
drivers when Berger explained
that he was still on a qualifying
lap and had not seen the
chequered flag indicating the
end of qualifying.*

MONZA

Alla fine gli encomiabili sforzi di
Michael Andretti sono stati ripagati
durante il Gran Premio d'Italia, tra
la felicità della folla di Monza che
ha parteggiato per lui: si è
aggiudicato un ben meritato terzo
posto e una qualifica sul podio di
Monza, sul quale suo padre era già
salito. Michael ha dovuto
contenderlo ancora alla Sauber di
Wendlinger; questa volta ha avuto
ragione dell'austriaco e lo ha
superato in terza posizione
entrando nella parabolica e
scivolandogli davanti in frenata.

The never ending efforts of
Michael Andretti finally paid off
during the Italian Grand Prix to
the delight of the partisan
Monza crowd netting him a well
deserved and very popular third
place and a position on the
sacred Monza podium where his
father once stood. Again Michael
had to contend with the Sauber
of Wendlinger, this time however
he came off better than the
Austrian and overtook him for
third position into the Parabolica
sliding past under braking.

MONZA

Nella pagina accanto:
Opposite:

Andrea De Cesaris, un altro pilota
aggressivo, quest'anno alla guida
della Tyrrell Yamaha, ha vissuto
nel Gran Premio di Monza
un'esperienza negativa, non
riuscendo mai a distinguersi nel
corso della gara di domenica.

Andrea De Cesaris, another
determined and aggressive driver
now driving the Tyrrel-Yamaha,
had a frustrating home Grand
Prix never really featuring in the
race come Sunday.

Blundell ha corso in sesta
posizione e avrebbe potuto
aspirare anche al podio; tuttavia
dopo il cambio delle gomme ha
preso la parabolica con traiettoria
troppo ampia e ha colpito la
barriera, forando una gomma e
interrompendo la sua risalita verso
le prime posizioni. Il suo
compagno di squadra, Martin
Brundle, è stato grossolanamente
spinto fuori da Senna, per un
errore di calcolo da parte del
brasiliano alla seconda chicane.

Blundell was running sixth and
in line for another podium,
however after a tyre stop he slid
wide at the Parabolica and hit
the barrier, puncturing his tyre
and ending his encouraging run
through the field. His team-mate
Martin Brundle was
unceremoniously punted off by
Senna, a miscalculation on the
Brazilians part at the second
chicane.

ESTORIL

Al dinamico ed esuberante
finlandese Mika Hakkinen, Ron
Dennis ha offerto finalmente
l'opportunità di dimostrare a tutti
di essere all'altezza della Formula
Uno. Egli, infatti, si è qualificato
meglio del suo illustre compagno
di squadra Ayrton Senna, risultato
che non si otteneva da due anni,
da quando cioè Gerhard Berger
era con il pilota brasiliano alla
McLaren. In più, Mika si è
mantenuto davanti a piloti esperti
come Senna, Prost, Schumacher
e Berger. É stato sorpassato solo
da Alesi, altro grintoso pilota
impegnato a dimostrare la sua
abilità nella rinnovata squadra
Ferrari.

*The dynamic and exuberant
Finn, Mika Hakkinen was
finally given the opportunity by
Ron Dennis to prove to all that
he belonged in Formula One.
He not only outqualified his
illustrious teammate Ayrton
Senna, a feat that has not been
achieved in two years since
Gerhard Berger partnered
Senna at McLaren, but Mika
then went on to lead such
luminaries as Senna, Prost,
Schumacher and Berger. He
was only headed by Alesi,
another young charger out to
prove his ability in the revived
Ferrari team.*

ESTORIL

Con il sostegno di quella che è
sembrata essere l'intera
popolazione portoghese, Pedro
Lamy, alla sua seconda gara di
Formula Uno e al primo Gran
Premio di casa, è stato spronato a
competere con impegno
veramente agonistico. La sua
guida decisa non ha deluso le
aspettative nel corso del Gran
Premio: si è mantenuto solo di
poche posizioni dietro al più
esperto compagno di squadra
Johnny Herbert; sfortunatamente
sono stati entrambi costretti a
ritirarsi in seguito all'incidente
avvenuto verso la fine della gara.
Pedro, comunque, ha certamente
mostrato a tutti di meritare un
ingaggio a tempo pieno.

*With the support of what
appeared to be the entire
Portuguese population, Pedro
Lamy competing in his second
Formula One event but first
home Grand Prix was under
immense pressure to perform.
He did not disappoint them
with a strong drive throughout
the Grand Prix only a few
places behind his more
experienced teammate Johnny
Herbert; unfortunately they
were both to retire due to
accidents towards the end of the
race, Pedro however had
certainly shown to everyone
that he deserves a full-time
drive.*

ESTORIL

Alain Prost ha soddisfatto ad Estoril le sue ambizioni e quelle della Renault, diventando il Campione del Mondo di Formula Uno 1993, suo quarto titolo e secondo per la Renault. Il suo fine settimana è stato comunque uno dei più avventurosi di tutta la stagione; durante le qualificazioni finali Alain ha subito un incidente ed è stato costretto a usare la macchina di Damon per gli ultimi minuti della sessione. Poche ore dopo, Prost ha annunciato il suo ritiro definitivo dalla Formula Uno, una sorpresa per tutti, inclusa la stampa, che ha convocato a un'improvvisa conferenza. La domenica lo si è visto relegato in quarta posizione sulla prima curva; è stato poi coinvolto in una dura ed emozionante contesa. La sua grande esperienza lo ha indotto a perseverare sulla distanza, diversamente dagli altri concorrenti, e gli ha permesso di raggiungere l'obiettivo della corona in Formula Uno per la quarta volta.

Alain Prost achieved his and Renaults 1993 ambition at Estoril by becoming the 1993 Formula One World Champion, his fourth title and Renaults second in succession. His weekend however was one of the most eventful he has had all season, during the final qualifying Alain crashed and had to use Damons car for the final minutes of the session. A few hours later, Prost announced his retirement from Formula One, a shock to everyone including the press, he called an impromptu press conference. Sunday saw him relegated to fourth by the first corner, he was in for a tough race, full of incident and excitement much needed in the sport. The professor lasted the distance unlike many of the others and achieved his goal of the Formula One crown for the fourth time.

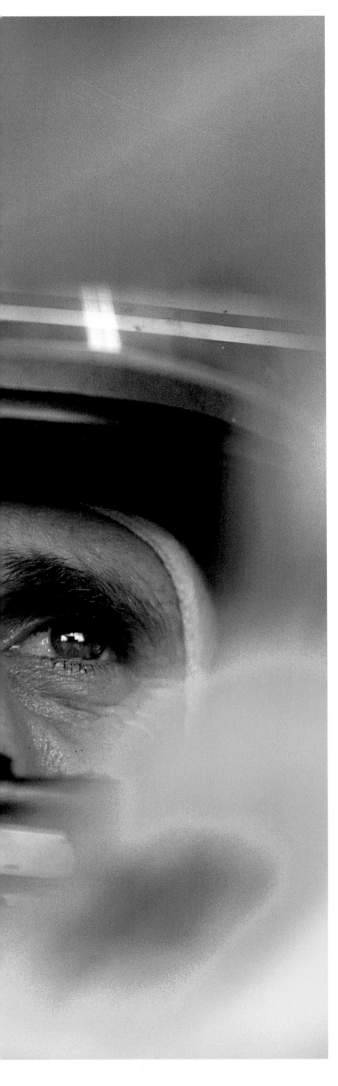

SUZUKA

A Suzuka Ayrton Senna ha
riportato una vittoria da vero
professionista. Il suo umore,
instabile come le condizioni
meteorologiche, gli ha permesso
di sfoderare determinazione e
grinta nell'attacco a Eddie Irvine.

*Ayrton Senna mastered the
changing weather conditions at
Suzuka a typically professional
win. However, just like the
weather Ayrton's mood was
changeable as he later attacked
new boy Eddie Irvine.*

SUZUKA

Mika Hakkinen ha continuato a
sostenere le speranze accese a
Estoril. Il Finlandese ha guidato in
maniera superba conquistando la
terza posizione e regalando alla
McLaren il suo miglior risultato
della stagione.

*Mika Hakkinen continued to
fulfil the promise shown at
Estoril. The flying Finn drove
superbly for 3rd position and
gave McLaren their best result
of the season.*

SUZUKA

Nella pagina accanto:
Opposite:

Berger, Schumacher e Hill hanno
iniziato a sfidarsi presto, ma solo
Hill era destinato ad arrivare fino
in fondo, concludendo la gara al
4° posto. Questo risultato è stato
comunque deludente per il pilota
inglese, che nei quattro
precedenti Gran Premi era
sempre salito sul podio.

*Berger, Schumacher and Hill do
battle early in the race. Only
Hill was destined to finish, 4th
position a disappointment for a
driver who's previous 4 Grand
Prix had resulted in podium
placings.*

SUZUKA

Volti nuovi a Suzuka: sul circuito sta salendo il sole e sotto ai suoi raggi brilla Eddie Irvine. Qualificatosi sempre fra i primi 10, questo debuttante ha fatto fremere i suoi tifosi giapponesi con un buon sesto posto. La sua allegria si è offuscata dopo la gara a causa di una discussione con Senna.

The new faces at Suzuka. Eddie Irvine shone in the land of the rising sun. Always posting qualifying times within the top 10 this debutant thrilled his enormous local following with a well deserved sixth place. Eddi's Joy was tarnished by Senna in a post race contretemps.

Jean-Marc Gounon, famoso per il suo controllo di guida nella Formula 3000, ha debuttato in Formula Uno con la Minardi.

Famed in International Formula 3000 for his superb car control, Jean-Marc Gounon struggled on his Formula 1 debut with Minardi.

Il pilota giapponese Toshio Suzuki, che ha sostituito Philippe Alliot alla Larrouse, ha potuto constatare quanto sia dura la vita in Formula Uno. Si è meritato di portare a termine la gara, sebbene con due giri di ritardo su Senna.

Japanese driver Toshio Suzuki replaced Philippe Alliot at Larrouse and found out how tough life is in Formula 1. He did gain credit for finishing the race albeit 2 laps behind Senna.

Aria di rinnovamento per la Ligier. La coloratissima auto guidata da Martin Brundle può essere considerata un'opera d'arte di Formula Uno, già esposta a una mostra a Monaco qualche tempo prima di Suzuka.

A new face-lift for Ligier. The cosmetic colourscheme piloted by Martin Brundle was an inspired piede of Formula 1 art, first seen at an exhibition in Monaco earlier in the year.

SUZUKA

Senna, sempre popolare in
Giappone, mostra la sua
soddisfazione sul podio. Il suo
pugno chiuso non solo
rappresenta un modo per rendere
partecipe la folla ma esprime
anche la sua rabbia nei confronti
di Eddie Irvine.

*Senna, always popular in
Japan, shows his delight on the
podium. His clenched fist was
used not only to acknoledge the
crowd but also to express his
frustrations on Eddie Irvine.*

ADELAIDE

In Australia la vittoria del Campionato di Formula Uno è ormai già decretata, così il Gran Premio di Adelaide finisce per essere spesso considerato un festoso appuntamento di fine stagione. In occasione della classica foto di fine Campionato Schumacher, Suzuki e Lehto sfoggiano il loro buon umore.

When the F1 Championship has already been won, many view Adelaide as an end of season party. In 1993 Schumacher, Suzuki and Lehto showed spirits were high at the annual end of season drivers photograph.

Spirito di squadra tra i piloti della Williams: Alain Prost ha scortato sul podio il suo compagno di squadra Hill durante la sua ultima corsa dopo 14 anni in Formula Uno.

Williams teamwork. Alain Prost lead home his teammate Hill in his last race after 14 years in Formula 1.

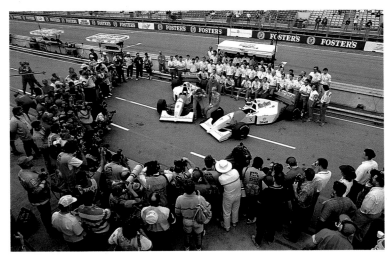

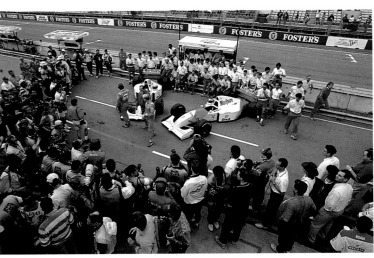

ADELAIDE

Scattare una foto a una squadra non vuol dire solo schiacciare il pulsante della macchina fotografica. Bisogna che le auto siano in posizione, così come le persone, cosa non facile quando si ha a che fare con personaggi come Ayrton Senna e il suo manager Ron Dennis.

Taking a team photograph is not simply about pressing a button on a camera. The cars need to be carefully set up in position then the photographer must arrange the personnel, not so easy when these include Ayrton Senna and his boss Ron Dennis.

ADELAIDE

Il quarto posto di Alesi ha rappresentato la ricompensa del duro lavoro in cui si sono impegnati tanto il pilota quanto tutta la squadra nel corso di un anno difficile.
(Nella pagina seguente)

4th place for Alesi was justification for all the hard work of both team and driver throughout a somewhat troublesome year.
(Following page)

ADELAIDE

Senna ha sostenuto una gara perfetta ad Adelaide, portando la sua McLaren alla vittoria: si è trattato della sua ultima corsa condotta con questa squadra le cui auto gli hanno fatto conquistare 3 Campionati del Mondo.
Con un gesto simbolico sul podio Senna e Prost dimenticano la loro ostilità e finalmente dimostrano il loro profondo rispetto reciproco.
Il terzo pilota, Damon Hill, dovrà scendere a patti con Senna perchè nel 1994 i due diventeranno compagni di squadra nella Williams.
(Nella pagina precedente)

Senna drove a perfect race in Adelaide, fittingly driving his McLaren to victory in his last race for a team who's cars have netted the Brazilian 3 World Championships.
In a symbolic gesture on the victory podium Senna and Prost forget their differences and finally acknowledge their mutual respect for one another's talents. The 3rd player, Damon Hill, will have to come to terms with Senna's skill as they become teammates at Williams for 1994.
(Preceding page)

ADELAIDE

Il quarto posto di Alesi ha rappresentato la ricompensa del duro lavoro in cui si sono impegnati tanto il pilota quanto tutta la squadra nel corso di un anno difficile.

4th place for Alesi was justification for all the hard work of both team and driver throughout a somewhat troublesome year.

DATA AND STATISTIC

olivetti

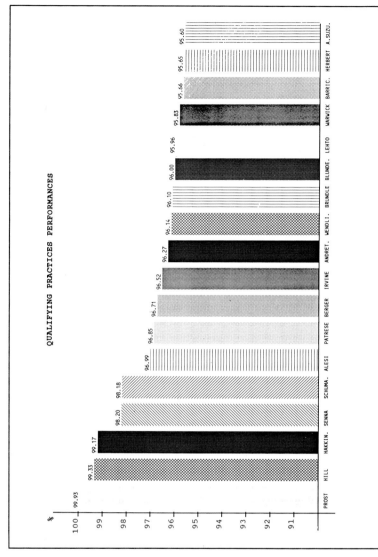

QUALIFYING PRACTICES PERFORMANCES

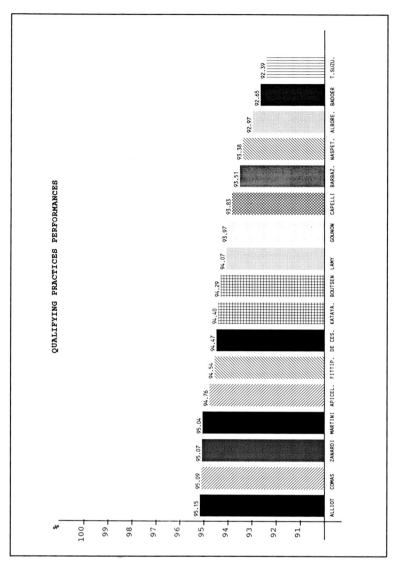

QUALIFYING PRACTICES PERFORMANCES

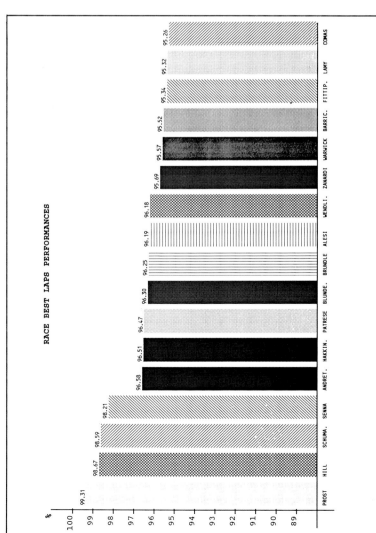

RACE BEST LAPS PERFORMANCES

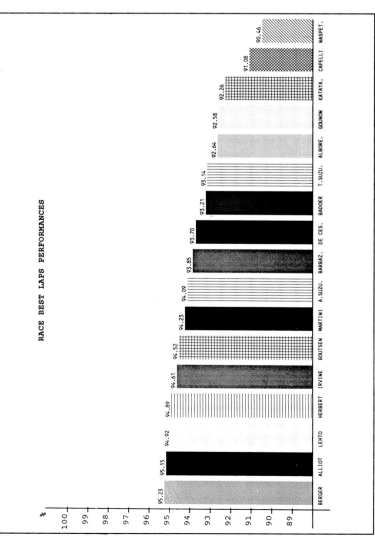

RACE BEST LAPS PERFORMANCES

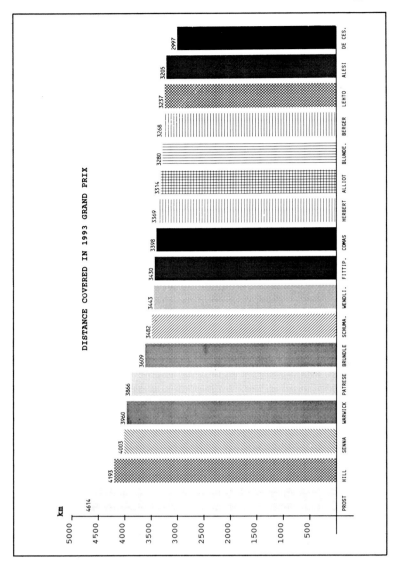

AVERAGE RACE SPEED IN 1993 GRAND PRIX
drivers with at least 8 races

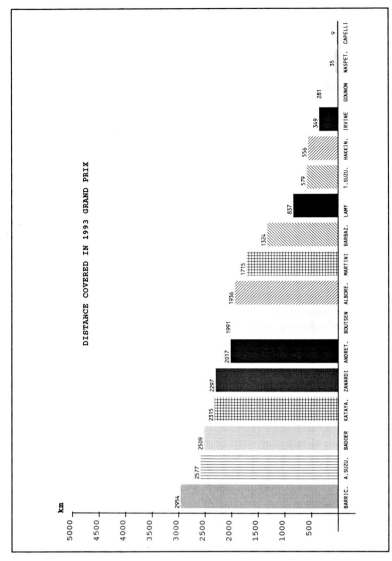

DISTANCE COVERED IN 1993 GRAND PRIX

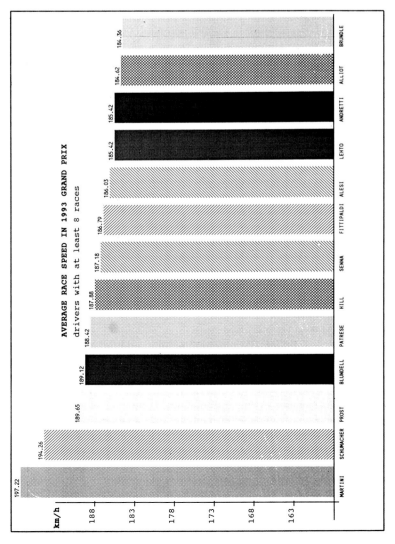

AVERAGE RACE SPEED IN 1993 GRAND PRIX
drivers with at least 8 races

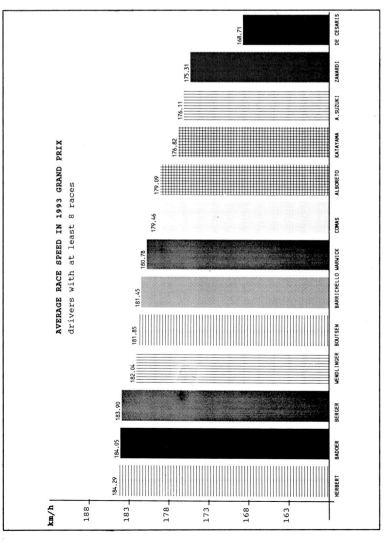

DISTANCE COVERED IN 1993 GRAND PRIX

DATA AND STATISTIC

olivetti

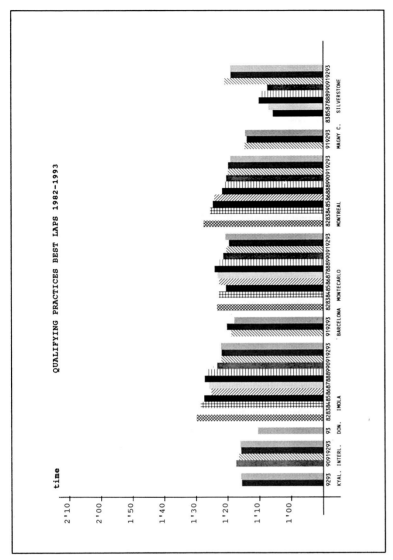

QUALIFYING PRACTICES BEST LAPS 1982-1993

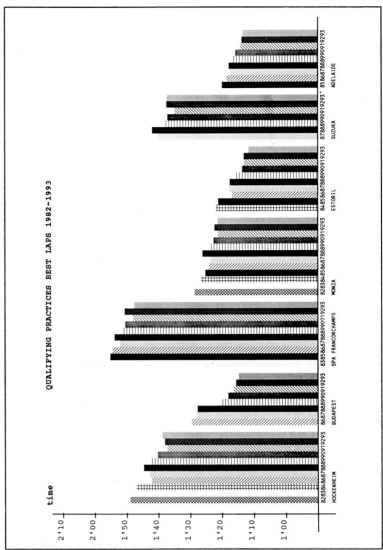

QUALIFYING PRACTICES BEST LAPS 1982-1993

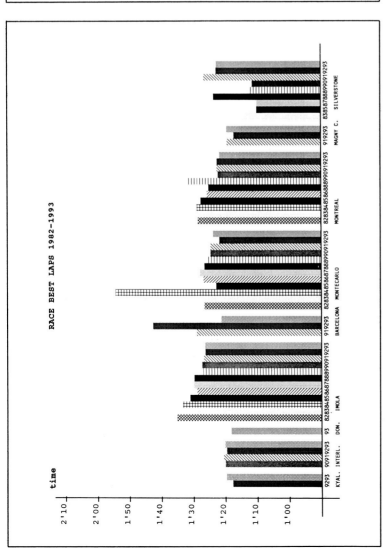

RACE BEST LAPS 1982-1993

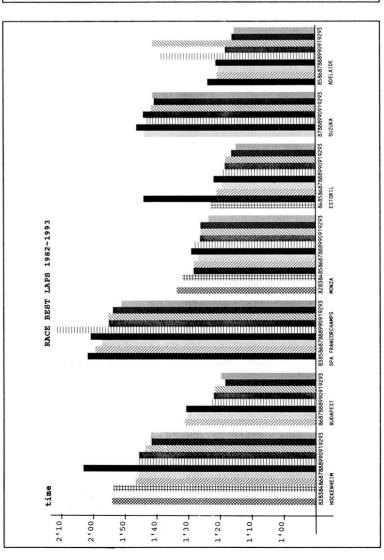

RACE BEST LAPS 1982-1993

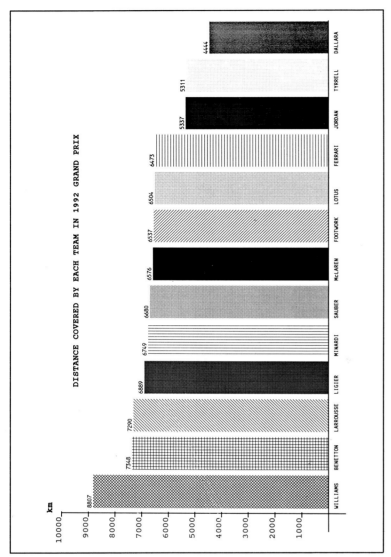

DISTANCE COVERED BY EACH TEAM IN 1992 GRAND PRIX

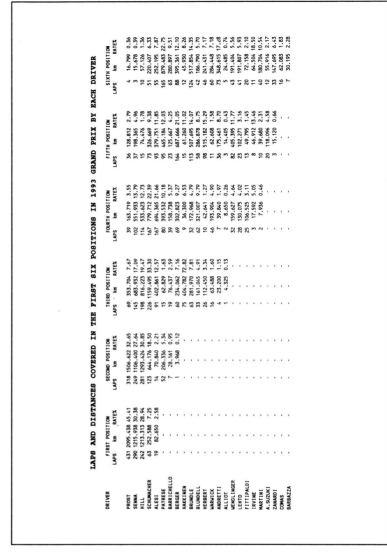

LAPS AND DISTANCES COVERED IN THE FIRST SIX POSITIONS IN 1993 GRAND PRIX BY EACH DRIVER

POINTS CLASSIFICATION

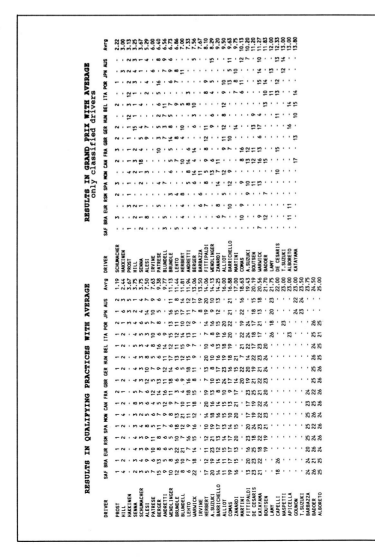

RESULTS IN QUALIFYING PRACTICES WITH AVERAGE

RESULTS IN GRAND PRIX WITH AVERAGE
only classified drivers

LAPS AND DISTANCES COVERED IN THE FIRST SIX POSITIONS IN 1993 GRAND PRIX BY EACH TEAM